'est
was
tain
the
ered
the University College of Wales at Aberystwyth from which he graduated in botany and economics.

It was a thoroughly good preparation for what lay ahead – 24 years in the seed industry, 20 of them with the Cuthbert Group. Now he is a freelance gardening writer and more heavily engaged than ever in his radio and TV work. For some 19 years he has been a panellist on the Welsh-language gardening programme on radio, as well as occasionally contributing to *Gardeners' Question Time*. He is also the presenter and performer on the half-hour television gardening programme on BBC Wales, and co-presenter, with Geoffrey Smith, of the BBC TV programme *Gardener's World*. In the past he has participated in the BBC's *Gardening Club* and *Dig This*, and in Border Television's gardening spot. He writes regularly for the gardening press.

A VEGETABLE PLOT FOR TWO – OR MORE

D. B. CLAY JONES

Illustrated by Ron Hayward

Hamlyn Paperbacks

A VEGETABLE PLOT FOR TWO – OR MORE

ISBN 0 600 39153 1

First published in Great Britain 1980
by Hamlyn Paperbacks

Hamlyn Paperbacks are published by
The Hamlyn Publishing Group Ltd,
Astronaut House,
Feltham,
Middlesex, England

Set, printed and bound in Great Britain by
Cox & Wyman Ltd., Reading

Cover photograph by Alan C. Squires

CONTENTS

INTRODUCTION

It is said that we grow wiser as we grow older. In other words, we gain experience with the passing years and we make fewer mistakes. This is certainly true in the realm of gardening, where the accumulation of knowledge, gleaned from literature and experience, leads to better and better results.

I caught the gardening bug at a very early age. I became fascinated by the mysteries of life and, in particular, life that is rooted in the soil. I thrilled to plants that responded to my ministrations and my failures served only as spurs to greater things. I made mistakes and learned from them. I quickly discovered a basic and simple truth – the more I knew about the plants in my garden, the better they grew. I studied their hardiness, their likes and dislikes, until I began to understand them, and, with greater understanding, came greater success.

The principle of understanding how plants live is of very special importance in the vegetable garden. Here we expect them to achieve a degree of performance far in excess of their natural inclination. We want maximum output from the minimum area. The extent to which our hopes are justified depends upon satisfying the needs of the plants to the full. We need to know which fertilizer benefits them most, whether they will grow in all kinds of soils, when to sow or plant them, when and how to harvest them, whether they are hardy or whether they need some kind of protection. All these things and more, point the way to a vegetable plot crammed full with good things to eat. I have written this book with just this objective in view – to help you to achieve the level of success that I have attained after several decades of trial and error.

I realize, of course, that not everyone has my unabated

enthusiasm for growing vegetables. There are those who consider it a waste of time, or too much trouble, or totally unprofitable. With respect, they are wrong. There are many very good reasons why you and I should grow our own vegetables. To begin with, it can be profitable, the extent of its profitability depending on many factors. To yield a high return on investment, the vegetable plot should provide food for the table during every week of the year, either fresh or from store. To the same end, every square metre of ground should be utilized to the full and not left bare if it can be planted to advantage.

Furthermore, the profitability is directly related to the amount of money spent on the necessities of good cultivation. We can forget tools as they are a once-in-a-lifetime investment. The recurring annual costs are, in the main, seed and fertilizers. Seeds are still comparatively inexpensive. A single packet of seeds of any vegetable is usually sufficient to provide a year's supply of fresh 'stuff' for the average family and the packet is not likely to cost more than about 20p at current prices. Just think of it, a hundredweight of carrots, or over half a hundredweight of runner beans, can be ours for less than it costs to buy a gallon of petrol – the difference in 'mileage' is appreciable! Fertilizers are admittedly more expensive and will become increasingly more so, but the wise gardener can cut his fertilizer costs dramatically by making his own compost – the natural manure that costs little and has everything.

To those who claim vegetable growing is a waste of time, I ask: how can anything that is productive be wasteful? In addition, tending the plot takes us out into the open air, to indulge in the gentle exercise of muscles that might otherwise 'run to seed'. It is a healthy pursuit as well as being productive. Vegetable growing is certainly not a lot of bother, there are few areas of the garden so undemanding of attention. There are periods of intense activity such as digging, sowing and planting, but these bursts of effort are short-lived and they need not be taxing in terms of time and physical endurance. The digging may – indeed should – be done during the winter months, a patch at a time, in leisurely fashion, over a period of several weeks. It only becomes a back-breaker if it is left to the last minute and has all to be done in a day or so.

The real rewards of growing our own vegetables lie in the freshness, flavour and cleanliness of home-grown produce. A vegetable, such as lettuce or cabbage, that has been freshly cut only minutes before it is eaten, tastes so much better than a specimen several days old bought from a shop. Of still greater importance is the fact that we have complete control over the vegetables we grow in our own gardens. It is we who decide which pesticides, if any, we wish to use to control insect pests and diseases. To me, this is a very important consideration. I have always felt that the indiscriminate and thoughtless use of chemical pesticides can be detrimental to human health and life, in the long term. My policy is to grow good strong plants in a fertile soil, so that they are constitutionally better able to withstand pest attack. I use pesticides only as a last resort, and, even then, only those that have been proved to be harmless to all but the pest being treated.

Lastly, by cultivating my own vegetable plot, I can choose which vegetable varieties I like best to grow and eat. Over the years I have grown almost every variety in the seedsmen's lists with varying degrees of satisfaction. My aim has always been to find the variety that yields the heaviest crop and at the same time possesses the finest flavour. This is often an unattainable goal and I sometimes have to sacrifice high yield in favour of taste. For example, if my only interest lay in total crop weight I would grow Moneymaker tomato, a variety that is way down the list for flavour. Instead, I grow the old Ailsa Craig and the newer Alicante for the sheer pleasure of sinking my teeth into tomatoes that ooze sweetness.

I hope the pages of this book will help you to select the best of the modern vegetable varieties and will assist you to grow them well and successfully. When you achieve this end you will find, like me, that vegetable gardening is more than a hobby – it becomes a way of life, packed with anticipation and pleasure.

D. B. Clay Jones

I

FIRST THINGS FIRST

For the purpose of this book I am assuming that you, the reader, know little, or nothing, about vegetable gardening. You may perhaps have recently acquired a garden for the first time, or you may have previously confined your gardening to growing ornamental plants. Now the situation is changed. Due to whim or necessity, you have an area of land on which you wish to grow vegetables. The questions that spring to mind are many. Is the area big enough? Is it suitable? What is the soil like? Will you be successful? These and other doubts assail you as you gaze at the proposed growing area.

Unwanted visitors

At this point you would be well advised to look around you. Before you begin to plan the plot, make sure that it will be impregnable and protected from at least some external and detrimental influences. If you live in a community, some of your neighbours are certain to have cats and dogs. They may well be lovable creatures, but they have an annoying habit of visiting neighbouring vegetable gardens, for a variety of infuriating reasons. Gardeners living in rural isolation are less troubled by cats and dogs, they have other problems. My mountainside garden is bordered by fields that are populated by cows, sheep, hares, rabbits and other domesticated and wild life. They all have one common aim – an insatiable desire to consume my vegetables before I do.

It is, therefore, necessary to put up a barrier to keep unwanted visitors out. A barrier can also serve another useful purpose: it can afford protection against the elements. In exposed gardens, strong winds can play havoc with some of the taller growing and tender leaved crops. After a strong gale I have seen Brussels sprouts and sprouting broccoli uprooted and lying flat on the ground, a total loss. On other occasions, rows of runner beans have had their leaves torn from their stems, just when they were about to start cropping. Such destruction is heartbreaking, because the loss is irreplaceable and another season must pass before you can try again. It is advisable to put up a barrier at the very beginning and avoid recrimination later on.

Initially the need is for a barrier that will afford instant protection from animals and the elements. The most impenetrable instant barrier is a fence consisting of sections of panelling, constructed of overlapping, or interwoven, strips of wood. The panels are held in place by stout posts driven into the ground, at intervals of about 2 metres (6 ft). The panels come in a variety of heights and the taller they are the more they cost. It is, therefore, a temptation to save money by buying the shorter panels. I would advise against such false economy as, although the 2-metre (6-ft) panels are a little more expensive, they are far more effective. A panelled fence is the last word in impenetrability, yet that very attribute can be its undoing. Such a fence presents a solid unyielding front to the prevailing winds, and, all too often, it gets blown down. It also calls for annual maintenance, in the form of painting with wood preservative to prevent it from rotting. All in all, a panelled fence is expensive to buy, it needs maintenance and, although a good barrier, it has no permanence.

Two-stage defence

Given the choice, I would opt for a cheaper, temporary barrier, to be followed by one that is both decorative and permanent. As my first line of defence I would put up a wire-netting fence with a mesh small enough to keep out the local troublemakers. Surprisingly, wire-netting also affords a fair amount of wind protection. Strong winds striking the mesh are broken up into smaller gusts and much of their power is dissipated. Having put the wire up, I would then immediately plant a living barrier on its inner side. There are many trees and shrubs that are ideal for hedging, but pause and consider

Wire netting fence with hedging on the inside

before you buy. The fastest growing 'hedger' is the Leyland cypress, *Cupressocyparis leylandii*. It is a conifer that grows at the rate of about 1 metre (3 ft) every year. It has much to commend it, as it is evergreen and densely leaved, thus affording year-round protection. But its rapid rate of growth is also its disadvantage, as it needs constant clipping to keep it under control. Also cats, dogs and other small animals can pass through it quite easily, at ground level. What is needed is a hedging plant that will permit no animal access and will afford good wind protection, whilst needing the minimum of upkeep. A quickthorn hedge meets all the criteria and it is also relatively inexpensive. Its branches grow closely together to form a close-knit barrier and they are thorny enough to repel the most determined tomcat. Quickthorn is deciduous and loses its leaves in the autumn, but by then the need for a wind barrier is much reduced, as there are fewer crops to protect. In any event, the quickthorn's closely interwoven branches are a good wind-resistant barrier in themselves.

There are also a number of hedging plants that are both protective and decorative. Several members of the berberis family are evergreen, and thorny, and they also burst into bloom in spring. *Berberis darwinii* and *B. stenophylla* make highly decorative hedges, being covered in April–May with bright orange-coloured blossom, followed by deep blue berries. Regular clipping, once a year, keeps them neat and tidy. As you would expect, berberis is a lot more expensive to buy than quickthorn, but, as a hedge is for life, it is worth spending a bit more to get what you want. Other useful and decorative hedging plants include beech – both the 'copper' and ordinary varieties, box (buxus), *Lonicera nitida*, shrub roses and pyracantha. For gardens near the sea, hedges must also be able to cope with salt-laden air, without having their leaves seared by summer gales. In a coastal situation, there is nothing to beat escallonia in its many varieties. The small, dark-green, glossy leaves form a dense, all the year round barrier and pale pink flowers clothe the hedge in summer.

Choosing a site

Having made sure that the crops you will be growing are protected from the elements, the next consideration is the actual site of the vegetable plot. It is, of course, almost certain to be at the back of the house. Most people wish to put their best front forward and in consequence front gardens are invariably ornamental. Here we have our rose beds and our annual and perennial flower borders, with perhaps a few flowering shrubs for company. I recall suggesting to a lady questioner on the *Gardeners' Question Time* radio programme, that she should plant her front garden with potatoes to clean the ground prior to sowing a new lawn. She stared at me in shock and disbelief. How could I suggest such a thing for a suburban garden? What would her neighbours think? Her reaction to growing vegetables in full sight of everyone was understandable, because tradition dies hard. Yet, vegetables are beautiful too, some being more beautiful than others.

Carrots and beetroot for instance have pretty leaves, and a few of them dotted here and there among the 'ornamentals' do not look out of place. Parsley makes a lovely edging plant, and many herbs, such as rosemary and borage, flower prettily in summer.

However, I accept that, for many reasons, the 'back' is the place for the vegetable plot. It allows one to work in comparative privacy and there is less danger of the crops being 'pinched' by passers-by, or judged by critical eyes. But wherever you decide to grow vegetables, aim for a site that gets as much sun as possible. There are very few vegetables that will crop even reasonably well in semi-shade and none that will produce anything in deep shade. Therefore site the plot where it will be the least affected by shadows cast by either the house, hedges, or tall trees. It is almost inevitable that parts of the back garden are in shadow during some periods in the day. If you can, choose a position where the plot will get as much sun as possible before midday. In my experience, all plants, including vegetables, make more use of the morning sun and grow faster before noon than they do afterwards.

Whenever possible avoid planting near trees and hedges. They cast shadows, but more importantly, they deprive the soil of two essential ingredients – water and plant food. The soil under and near trees and shrubs is drier than anywhere else in the garden. Their roots absorb vast quantities of water to compensate for moisture loss through the leaves and when it rains, their dense foliage prevents much of the rain from falling on the soil below. It should also be remembered that plants cannot eat, they can only drink. Therefore, in a dry soil, they are deprived, not only of water, but also of the plant food that the water contains. In some gardens, it is either impossible, or impracticable, to avoid part of the vegetable plot, at least, being near or under trees and shrubs. In such a situation, the affected area will need more fertilizer and many times more water than other areas further removed from the influence of trees and shrubs. It is also advisable, though not essential, that the rows of vegetables should run from north to south. Arranged in this fashion, both sides of the rows receive a fair share of sunshine, as the sun passes over them on an east to west course. Bearing this in mind and remembering that vegetable plots are usually longer than they are broad, site the plot so that its long sides run from east to west and its short sides from north to south.

Plot size

The size of the vegetable plot depends, to a degree, on the available ground. The enthusiast will aim to keep his family and himself supplied with produce from one year's end to the next. He will be looking for up to 2000 sq. metres (half an acre) of ground and he will grow everything including early and maincrop potatoes. Most gardeners have to make do with a much smaller garden, but even in the depths of suburbia it is usually possible to devote a piece of ground measuring 12 × 4.5 metres (40 × 15 ft), a total of 54 sq. metres (600 sq. ft), to vegetable growing. While this is a comparatively small plot, by careful planning and cropping, it can provide something fresh for the table from January to December.

Bird's eye view

Having decided on the site and size of the plot, it is time to climb the stairs to the back bedroom armed with paper and pencil. It is easier to plan a garden from above than it is at ground level. A bird's eye view brings all existing boundaries and features into better proportion. In your mind's eye, and with a little imagination, you can see the garden as it will look when your plans are completed. Begin by marking existing features on to the plan, then add other features that you may wish to include, such as a compost heap, a greenhouse, a garden frame or a shed. Lastly, pencil in the vegetable plot, after which you may find you will have to start all over again, because you have forgotten all about paths.

PATH MAKING

Adequate, convenient paths are very important. They should be wide enough to allow for humping around barrow-loads of muck and other mysteries and they should provide for easy, direct access to all parts of the plot and to the various focal points. There is little use, for instance, in having a compost heap, if you have to trample over rows of potatoes to get to it. Besides being wide, paths should also provide a firm, clean and stable surface. They can be of hard-trodden earth, grass, paving-slabs, tarmac, gravel, clinker or ash.

Paving-slabs may sometimes be obtained cheaply, if you are fortunate enough to find your Local Authority tearing up stretches of pavement. Have a quiet word with the foreman and suggest to him that you are prepared to pay for the removal of the broken slabs, to save him the embarrassment of finding somewhere to dump them. You could be lucky! If you are, make sure you lay them well because they will last a lifetime. First of all, rake the ground level and set the slabs with a half-inch space between them. Leave them for a week or two to settle in and reset any that are jutting up above, or have sunk below, the predetermined level. Then concrete between the slabs to bind them to a permanent, immovable path. To prevent the soil from falling on to the path and to finish the job off tidily, the path can be bounded with lengths of precast concrete edging, placed in position before the slabs are laid. The concrete edging can usually be obtained from most builders' yards at fairly low cost. I am not enamoured of gravel, clinker, or ash paths. The stuff sticks to the soil on my boots and 'wellies' and wheeling a barrow over it can be hard work. Grass paths look nice, but need constant care in summer. They have to be mown and their edges have to be clipped at least once a week, for the best part of the year. They also wear with constant use, leaving a bald strip down the middle which becomes a muddy squelch in wet weather. The bare patches can be avoided by sinking stepping stones, or slabs, all down the centre of the paths, but they still need mowing and clipping. Tarmac paths are excellent if you can find a ready source of material. Their main drawback is that they become skating-rinks in frosty weather and can be quite slippery in wet weather. My own preference is for a hard-trodden, earth path edged with concrete. It makes a comparatively clean, non-skid surface and costs nothing except for the concrete edging strips. Earth paths were once unpopular because they became covered with weeds and needed constant cleaning. Nowadays, a single application of a simazine-based, path weedkiller, applied in March, will keep them weed-free for a whole season.

Siting your greenhouse

To recap, we now have our plot marked out on the ground and we have established our paths around it. Now where are we going to site our greenhouse and the other bits and pieces? Like the vegetable rows and for the same reasons, the greenhouse should have all the sun that is going, and it should be so positioned that its length runs from north to south. Bearing in mind that most greenhouses are glass structures, keep yours well away from trees and avoid breakages caused by falling twigs and branches. Before finally deciding where to put it, consider two things: greenhouse plants need a lot of water in summer and heat in winter. So it could be worthwhile running underground water and electricity supplies to the greenhouse before you establish your paths and have to dig them up again. Even if you intend to heat the greenhouse with paraffin, oil or solid fuel, electricity is still a boon. It provides light to work by of an evening and it can be used to heat a propagator for the germination of seeds and the striking of cuttings. I do suggest, however, that you have the electrical installation done professionally, to avoid the possibility of shocking accidents later on.

The positioning of the greenhouse decides where you put the garden frame. As the frame is used, among other things, for hardening off soft-grown greenhouse plants prior to planting out, it is convenient to have it right alongside. The compost bin can go anywhere. Some prefer to site it near the back door for sheer convenience. Others tuck it away, out of sight, in the furthest corner of the garden, on the grounds that it is unsightly and obnoxious. In reality, many of the modern, plastic compost bins are not unattractive and if the bin is working properly, there is no offensive smell. You can compromise by having a small lidded bin outside the back door, wherein to dump kitchen waste. When it is full, the waste is transferred to the compost bin at the far end of the garden and everyone is happy.

A garden shed

Where a garden shed is concerned, think before you buy. Do you really need one? In a small garden a shed occupies valuable space that could well be used for growing things. If you have a garage, there is usually enough space to accommodate garden tools and the accessories that gardeners tend to accumulate. But if your garden can take it, a shed is extremely useful. It becomes a tool-shed, a potting-shed and a hide-out when things get on top of you. Site it at the furthermost part of the garden, where you can work, or idle, in peace and utter contentment.

TOOLS

Next comes the question of tools. Without doubt, you should always buy the best because, in the long run, they are the cheapest. A good implement lasts a lifetime and makes light of hard work. I recall going to a village to give a gardening talk and meeting an elderly gentleman who had brought along his trusty spade to show me. He had bought it in 1923, used it regularly every year since and 55 years later it was almost as good as new. He paid 12*s*. 6*d*. (or 62½p) for it in those far off days, when you could buy a spade of sorts for 2*s*. 6*d*. (or 12½p). He told me how he had resisted the temptation to buy a cheap tool and how he had put by 6*d*. (or 2½p) every week until he could afford the spade that was to be his constant companion in over 50 years of gardening. He was glad he had bought the best and so will you be.

A full set of good tools for the vegetable plot can be very expensive if they all have to be purchased at the same time. In order to help people who are totally unequipped, I suggest they buy their tools in three phases: the essentials, the necessities and the desirables.

The essentials

A spade must be the very first consideration. At the top end of the price scale are the stainless steel spades that cost almost ten times as much as the cheapest models. A stainless steel spade is a beautiful tool to own, to look at and to use, but it is a luxury that few of us can afford. I suggest that a young couple about to get married should include one on their 'list of presents'; they could be lucky if they have a rich relative who is also a keen gardener. If they have to buy their own, they should seek out a spade with a strong steel blade, securely fixed to a stout ash, or fibre-glass, handle. Choose the handle with care, for it comes with two different grips – a 'T' grip and what I shall call a 'closed U' grip. Of the two I prefer the latter because it allows for a firmer hold on the handle. The 'T' grip necessitates having two fingers on either side of the handle which reduces the firmness of one's hold. Finally, having selected what appears to be a good tool, try it for weight, width and balance, in the shop. If it feels part of you, it is your spade – buy it.

A good fork is the second essential. Indeed, if your soil is heavy clay it may be wise to buy the fork before the spade. It is a lot easier to dig a heavy clay soil with a fork than with a spade. A fork also comes in handy for manhandling manure and compost, bashing and breaking up large clods of clay, digging up potatoes and for sundry other jobs. When buying, the same criteria apply as for buying a spade – get a good one that suits you down to the tips of its prongs.

When it comes to buying a rake there is a world of difference between the good and the bad. The rake to avoid is the one that looks as though it has nails for teeth. The nails, or prongs, have blunt, rounded ends that easily clog with soil. They also have a habit of working loose and of getting bent and misshapen. A good rake has a one-piece, steel head with sharp-pointed prongs that can rapidly reduce soil to a fine texture or tilth. Check the handle also and select one that is straight and made of well-seasoned wood, or fibre-glass, that will not warp.

In basic construction there are two kinds of hoe, the Dutch hoe and the draw-hoe. Both have their uses in the vegetable plot, but if I had to choose between them I would class the Dutch hoe as essential and the draw-hoe as necessary. The Dutch type looks like a pitchfork with a blade between the tips of the two prongs. It is the ideal tool for hoeing off weeds between rows of vegetables, on paths and on vacant ground, prior to sowing and planting. When using it you start at the top end of the plot and work backwards, severing and uprooting the weeds as you go. The weeds are left lying on the loosened soil, to shrivel in the sun, or they may be raked up and put on the compost heap.

The draw-hoe has two uses, as a weeder and as a seed-drill maker. For weed killing it has a disadvantage over the Dutch hoe in that the user walks forward over the hoed ground. He treads on the uprooted weeds and unless they are raked up, many of them will re-root. When drawing out seed drills, a corner of the blade, which is at right angles to the handle, is pushed into the soil and drawn along a taut garden line to make a shallow furrow. However, if you can only afford to buy one hoe at a time, you can still draw out seed drills using a blunt corner of the rake head, without having to acquire a draw-hoe for the purpose.

When shopping for either kind of hoe choose ones with good handles and strong steel heads that are no more than 7 to 10 cm (3 to 4 in.) wide. I prefer a 7-cm (3-in.) wide blade because it is easier to use between close-growing rows of vegetables, such as onions and lettuce, without getting too near the plants and damaging the lateral roots.

Other bits and pieces that are essential to every vegetable gardener are a hand trowel for planting, a good sharp knife, a garden line, a watering can and a quantity of bamboo canes of varying length. The line need cost very little. All that is required is a length of strong twine or nylon cord, at least half as long again as the longest row length and two stout stakes about 38 cm (15 in.) long. Drill a hole in each stake, about 2 cm from the top end, pass the cord through and knot it, to prevent it slipping back. Sharpen the other ends of the stakes to facilitate pushing them into the soil and you have a good garden line.

If you live in the country you may not have to buy bamboo canes. The hedges abound with stakes and twiggy sticks, that are ideal for supporting crops such as runner beans and peas. Most farmers who own the hedges are willing to let you have a few bundles of sticks, but do ask them first. If you have no alternative but to buy canes, look after them and they will last for several years. When their job is done, pull them out of the ground, wipe them clean, tie them in bundles according to size and store them in a dry shed or garage.

A watering can is also an essential adjunct to vegetable gardening, whether you have a greenhouse or not. In the plot itself, cabbage plants and the like need watering-in after planting, and during long, dry spells the whole plot requires watering to maintain a good rate of growth. Nowadays, cans are available in metal and plastic material. Of the two I prefer the plastic cans because they are rustproof and virtually indestructible. For the family vegetable plot, get a can of 9 litres (2 gallons) capacity with, if possible, two 'roses' (a 'rose' is the perforated attachment through which the water emerges). A rose with large-sized perforations is ideal for watering young and established plants, whereas newly sown seed trays and small seedlings should be watered with a finely perforated rose to avoid disturbance and damage. So choose your watering can carefully and, having chosen, buy two. This seeming extravagance is in fact a wise precaution. One can is used for normal watering, the other is allotted the job of weedkilling and should be suitably and prominently marked to denote its function. By having two cans, there should be little danger of destroying your prized vegetables by watering them with toxic chemicals that the can may have previously contained.

The necessities

The essentials enable you to start your vegetable growing programme, the necessities are the tools to greater fulfilment and success. A mattock, and the similar Chillington hoe, have numerous uses and they are especially useful on hard, heavy ground. They are wielded from above and behind, to bring the business end of the tool down, with great force, to break through clay soil and to cut through tree roots and so on. They can also be employed for ridging and for earthing and unearthing potatoes. Another cultivating tool that I would never be without is a long-handled shovel, often called a Cardiganshire or Welsh shovel. It has a long, slightly arched handle and a heart-shaped metal blade. It is a great tool for opening and closing trenches, earthing, shovelling and as

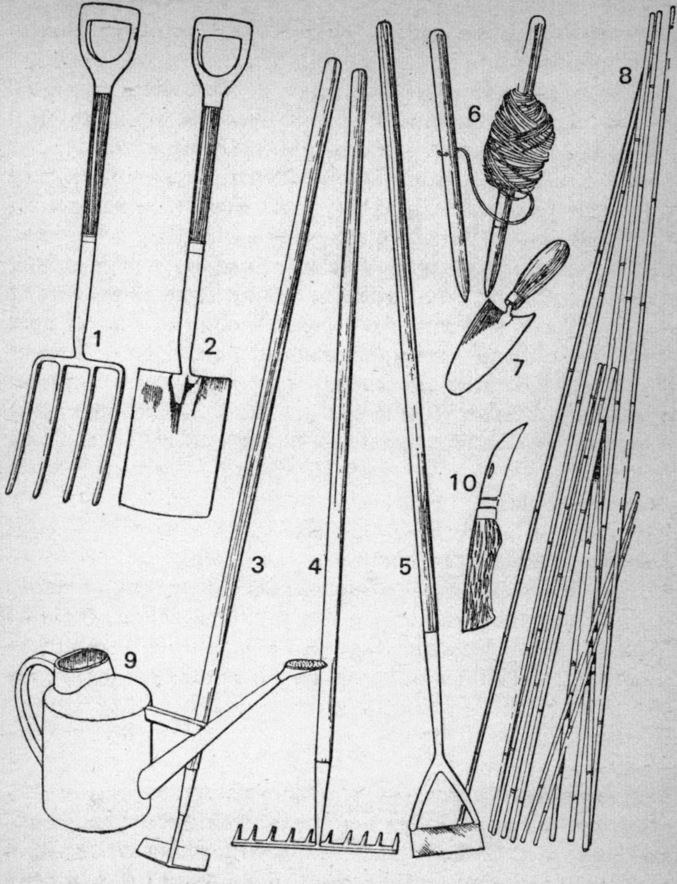

Garden tools: 1 digging fork, 2 digging spade, 3 draw hoe, 4 rake, 5 Dutch hoe, 6 garden line, 7 hand trowel, 8 bamboo canes, 9 watering can, 10 pruning knife

the handle fits snugly under the armpit, just for leaning on!

A hand fork is handy for yanking out reluctant weeds and a dibber comes in useful for levering seedlings out of seed trays and for pricking out. Frankly, I have never owned a dibber as I find that the blunt end of a pencil, or a spent, disposable ball-point pen will do just as well. A wheelbarrow is another necessity, for obvious reasons. I have not classed it as essential, as you can make do with an opened-out sack for carting stuff around, until adequate funds allow for the purchase of a barrow. For small gardens, where there is little humping to be done, a low-priced, solid-tyred, aluminium wheelbarrow will prove adequate. But for large gardens, sloping ground and much conveying of muck and other matter, a large vehicle with a pneumatic-tyred wheel makes for easier trundling. In my day I have gardened in old shoes, 'wellies' and boots, and, without doubt, a strong, thick-soled pair of boots is best. Boots make digging easier, they wear well and they support and aerate the feet. The last of the necessities are cloches of which more is written in another chapter.

The desirables

Desirables are tools and equipment that we yearn to possess, but can seldom afford in our early gardening years. A greenhouse is the most expensive item in the garden, yet the return from it cannot be counted in monetary terms alone. It makes for an almost endless growing season, it is a warm retreat in the dark depths of winter and properly used, it can pay for itself in two years or so. If you get a greenhouse, then of course you need a 'frame' to go with it, but more about under-cover gardening later on.

Every gardener worthy of the name, should have at least one compost heap somewhere near the vegetable plot. Bins for the purpose are many and readily available, but they are desirable rather than essential. For years I made beautiful, rich compost by merely throwing organic waste into a hole in the ground and covering it with a sheet of polythene. During this period my gardening knife was my constant companion. Now it shares a pocket with a pair of sharp-edged, anvil-action secateurs. The latter is used mainly on fruit trees, roses and for general pruning, but it often comes in useful in the vegetable plot as well.

The final 'desirable' that borders on a necessity is a garden hose. During protracted spells of very dry weather, vegetables need large quantities of water. At such a time a watering can, though better than nothing, is scarcely adequate. What the plot needs is a thorough soaking that can only be provided by a hose with a sprinkler attachment.

You will have noticed that I have not included an incinerator anywhere in my list of tools. The omission is deliberate as the average household and garden should have nothing to burn. All organic waste, from the garden and the kitchen, is a potential source of valuable fertilizer and it all goes on the compost heap.

I stress again that good quality tools add greatly to the pleasure of working in the garden and that cheapness is akin to false economy.

2

GETTING THE BALANCE RIGHT

When one is restricted to a vegetable plot measuring 12 × 4.5 sq. metres (40 × 15 ft), there are limits to the number of different vegetables that can be grown and to the number of rows of each kind. Therefore, it is essential to plan very carefully in order to derive the maximum satisfaction from every square metre of ground. Consideration should be given to the likes and dislikes of every member of the family to try to arrive at a well-balanced selection of vegetables and varieties. I suggest the following criteria as useful guidelines. The first criterion is enjoyment. I eat and enjoy all vegetables without exception, but, like most people, I enjoy some more than others. My favourites, and my wife's, are the ones that have top priority and the most rows.

Which crops to grow?

The second criterion is cost and there are two aspects to bear in mind. Where space is at a premium it pays to concentrate on the vegetables that are the most expensive to buy. Peas and beans, for instance, maintain a fairly high shop price throughout the season. Furthermore, it grieves me to pay many pence for a pound of broad beans, shell them, and throw most of my purchase on the compost heap. On the other hand, summer cabbages are always reasonably cheap to buy. Our aim, therefore, should be to grow those vegetables that give the highest return, in value, from the ground they occupy. Secondly, some vegetables take up a lot more space than others. Rows of carrots and beetroot need not be more than 30 cm (1 ft) apart, whereas potatoes need a spacing of about 60 cm (2 ft) and bush marrows as much as 90 to 120 cm (3 to 4 ft) from plant to plant.

So here again you have to weigh your personal preferences against the yield per unit area of ground. Potatoes are another prime example of the value to space ratio. Early new potatoes are expensive in the shops, but they soon come down in price as the season advances and supplies become more plentiful. In a smallish plot, therefore, I would grow only one or two rows of early potatoes, partly on cost consideration and partly because they taste so good, cooked and eaten straight out of the ground. I would not grow maincrops at all, as commercially grown potatoes are of good quality and inexpensive.

Freshness

The third criterion is freshness. All vegetables have a fuller, finer flavour when they are eaten only minutes after harvesting. This applies in particular to soft-leaved and podded vegetables. Things like lettuces and peas rapidly lose their delicate flavour after cutting and picking, and, in addition, lettuces also lose their lovely, crisp texture. Root vegetables retain their taste for several months, but even they are sweeter and juicier when they are young and tender. A young, 7-cm (3-in.) long carrot pulled and eaten in midsummer tastes very different to a mature carrot eaten from store in midwinter. So, where you have to choose what you grow, sow and plant the vegetables that are the first to lose their flavour and texture after leaving the ground.

Knowledge and experience

The fourth criterion is your own knowledge and experience. Provided the soil is fertile, there are lots of vegetables that are easy to grow to an acceptable standard. There are others that require greater expertise and more constant attention. Also, some vegetables are more prone to pest problems than others, and unless you are prepared to learn to recognize and deal with the invaders it might be advisable to leave these alone until you are more experienced. Having given this warning, let me add that there is no vegetable that is too difficult for the amateur gardener to grow successfully. All that is necessary is a fertile soil and the kind of knowledge that can be gleaned from numerous sources, of which this book is one.

Supply and demand

The fifth and final criterion concerns supply and demand. In our household there is a constant demand for vegetables on every day of the year. Our aim, therefore, is to meet the demand within the limits of the plot's ability to provide an all-the-year-round supply. To be entirely self-sufficient a family of four, who eat moderately rather than gluttonously, would need at least 1000 sq. metres (a quarter of an acre) of ground to keep themselves in 'veg' from the year's beginning to its end. It is beyond the bounds of our space-restricted plot to provide such a year-round supply. Nevertheless, by careful planning, it is possible to enjoy at least one home-grown vegetable every week of the year. In summer, fresh garden produce is plentiful and there may even be a glut of some vegetables, unless we have chosen and planted wisely. In winter, the well-planned plot should provide Brussels sprouts, winter cabbage, leeks and parsnips – all hardy vegetables that can withstand the severest weather. There should also be quantities of root crops that were lifted in the autumn and stored for winter use – carrots, beetroot and swedes for instance. In a later chapter you will find a table (*see* pp. 72 to 77) giving sowing and planting dates and the season of use of all the vegetables that are normally grown in Britain.

Crop rotation

There is one further consideration that decides where different vegetables are to be grown in the plot. This is because vegetables, like gardeners, appreciate a change now and again. It has long since been recognized that certain vegetables tend to deteriorate when grown in the same piece of ground year after year. There are two reasons for this. Firstly, different vegetable groups have different fixed diets. They always use up the same plant foods from the soil – more of some and less of others. This life-style leads to an imbalance of soil nutrients if the same vegetable groups always occupy the same soil areas. Root crops for instance need larger quantities of phosphates than do peas and beans and leafy crops require comparatively high quantities of nitrogen or nitrates. Furthermore, all members of the peas and beans family (the legumes) have the

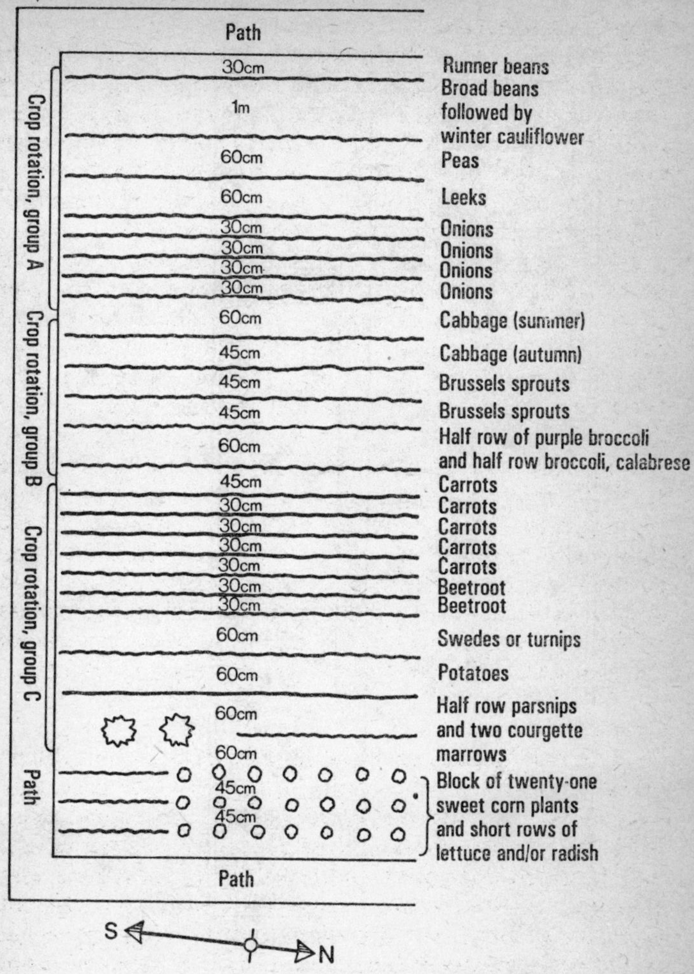

Plan of vegetable plot showing rows, etc.

ability to produce nitrogen in their roots, so that the ground they have occupied may have some residual nitrogen left in. Secondly, each vegetable group, or family, is susceptible to attack by certain insect pests and diseases. All members of the

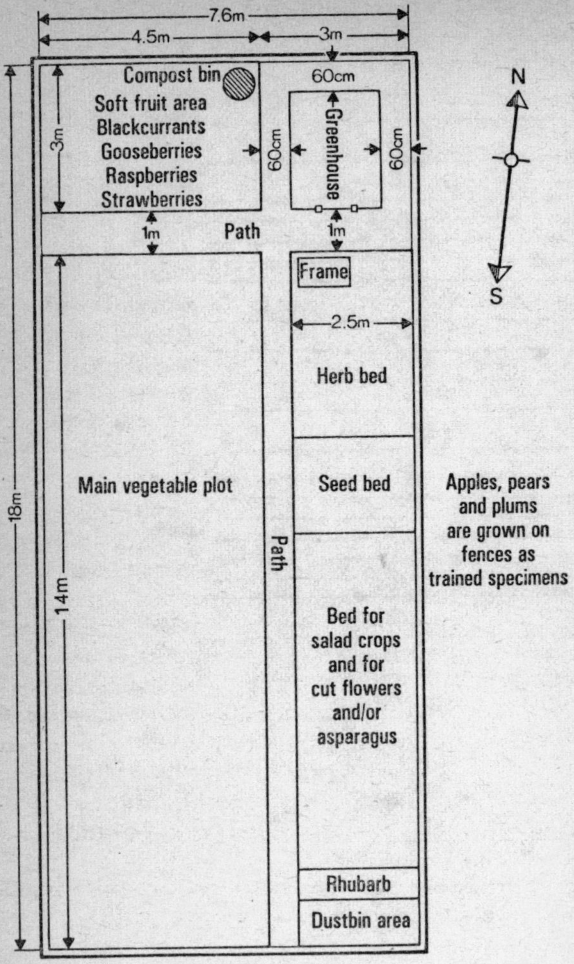

Plan of back garden layout

cabbage family, for instance, are assailed by grubs of the cabbage root fly and this pest can overwinter in the soil from one year to the next. Grown in the same patch, year after year, cabbages become increasingly vulnerable as the pest population builds up. The same is true of many other pests and diseases, which is why it pays to move vegetable groups to new areas of the plot in successive years.

The movement of vegetable groups around the plot is called crop rotation. To practise a simple and effective crop rotation system, it is necessary to segregate vegetables into three major groups. These are the legumes, or all members of the peas and beans family; the brassicas, or all members of the cabbage family; and the root crops, such as carrots, potatoes, beetroot, parsnips, swedes and turnips. This leaves a few vegetables without an appropriate grouping. Purely for convenience, I group leeks and onions with the legumes and anything else gets grown wherever there is ground available. The layout plan of the plot on p. 19 illustrates the way in which I would distribute the vegetable groups in the first year. In the second and succeeding years the groups move one pace to the left, so that the brassicas follow legumes, root crops follow brassicas and legumes follow root crops. If you practise such a simple rotation programme, you will have better and healthier crops.

The plan of the main vegetable plot also reflects our own personal preferences for particular vegetables. For example, I have allowed for five rows of carrots, because we like them and because they will keep in store for six months or more. We are not mad keen on parsnips and half a row is all we need. The plan caters for the cultivation of 18 different vegetables. You may wish to grow more or fewer kinds and more or fewer rows of each kind; therefore the plan has to be flexible to meet your own requirements. Whatever you decide, try to keep to the grouping and take the row spacings as being the ideal in a soil of average fertility.

The second plan on p. 20 suggests how a growing area measuring 18 × 7 metres (60 × 25 ft) may be utilized to best advantage. It is a simple, no-nonsense layout that makes for easy maintenance, gives adequate row lengths and includes all that is desired in an amateur's productive plot – fruit and vegetables in plenty.

3

LOOKING AFTER THE SOIL

This is the most important chapter in the book. Without knowledge of the nature of the soil and of its fertility, there is no hope of growing plants successfully. It is one of the essential ingredients of life itself, as vital to our continued existence as are air and water. Everything we eat derives directly, or indirectly, from the thin veneer of soil that covers the Earth. Should it ever lose its fertility, or become toxic to plant life, all living things, plants and animals would perish. It would seem, therefore, that Man's prime objective would be the maintenance of that which provides for his very existence – the soil. Yet, over the centuries, Man has treated the soil with scant respect. Today there are vast man-made areas of barren waste on the American continent and elsewhere, that are the outcome of our inability to understand soil and to perpetuate its fertility. Fortunately, we who now grow things, gardeners and farmers alike, are beginning to comprehend the true function and constitution of the soil that is our staff of life.

We know that good soil, that will grow good plants, is, on average, no more than 30 cm (1 ft) deep. Below this layer of topsoil, lies a varying depth of subsoil that is virtually lifeless and is composed mainly of inert clay. Below this again lies an impenetrable depth of unyielding shale and rock. If we are to understand the nature and composition of the topsoil, we have to combine fact and theory as to its origins. It seems certain that at its birth, many millions of years ago, our world was a rocky sphere totally devoid of soil or life. It existed, however, in a corrosive atmosphere. In other words, its surface was under constant bombardment by wind, rain and heat, that sanded it down to dust. Then, by chance, or superhuman design, life appeared in the form of microscopic, unicellular organisms. It wasn't much, but it was the beginning from which all subsequent life forms have sprung.

The great secret of life is its mortality. All living things die and, in death, provide for future life. Over countless time the plants and animals that have populated the world have each perished and their bodies have decomposed and merged into the Earth's crust. The result of timeless decay is the topsoil – a mixture of finely ground rock particles and decomposed animal and vegetable matter, the one inorganic and the other organic. In these two words, inorganic and organic, lie the secrets of soil fertility. Inorganic matter is purely chemical and inert. In contrast, organic matter, in gardening terms, refers to material that is either alive or has known life. It now becomes apparent that, in order to maintain soil fertility, we must uphold the natural ratio of its inorganic and organic content.

At this point we pause and review past history. In the early days of Man's existence he took what Nature haphazardly provided. He fed off the plants and animals that were close at hand and, when his local food supply became exhausted, he moved on in search of fresh supplies. All other animals followed a similar life pattern and there existed a natural equilibrium. This happy state of affairs could have continued indefinitely but for one shattering change – Man was given, or he acquired, supremacy over all other forms of life. He developed the power of thought – a valuable and perhaps dubious asset. What has this to do with soil fertility? The answer is that the faculty of thought revolutionized Man's way of life. He ceased his wanderings in search of food and instead established himself in a fixed area where he set about dictating terms to Nature. He began to exercise control over growth. He cleared areas of jungle and sowed and planted his choice of plants. In short, Nature's life equilibrium was upset for the first time in the Earth's history, as Man began to take more out of the soil than he put back in.

This brings us to the second great gardening lesson, you only get out of the soil what you put into it; which leads us to Man's next, near catastrophic, meddling with natural equilibrium.

In the mid-nineteenth century scientists discovered that plants relied heavily on certain chemical elements for their health and growth. These elements occur naturally throughout the whole of the plant and animal kingdoms and they are also available in purely chemical forms. Therefore, the scientists surmised that plants could be fed by chemical elements alone and so began the massive industry that has since produced vast quantities of artificial, chemical fertilizers.

Gardeners and farmers took to the new fertilizers with enthusiasm. In their concentrated, chemical form they were cleaner than manure and a lot easier and lighter to handle. In place of the barrowloads of manure he had been wheeling around, the gardener found he could use a few kilos of 'artificials' instead. There was only one thing wrong with this new and convenient fertility system. It provided food for the plants but it contributed nothing to the basic structure of the soil. As its organic content decreased, it lost its cohesive powers. It became an unsubstantial rooting medium that, in some areas, just blew away in the wind. Also as the soil's cohesion fell, so did its ability to retain nutritional elements in solution. As a result, the more gardeners used, and still use, inorganic fertilizers in isolation, the less benefit they or their plants derived from them. With the soil's holding capacity depleted, much of the soluble inorganic elements leach away before plants can use them.

It is now obvious that soil fertility is a dual operation. On the one hand it needs organic matter to uphold its structure and cohesion and it needs certain chemical elements to provide for plant growth. In addition, organic matter also maintains the bacterial population of the soil at the right level. These are the beneficial bacteria that are necessary in a rich, buoyant soil. The question is, are organic natural fertilizers sufficient in themselves, or do they need boosting with 'inorganics'? There are knowledgeable and professional gardeners who preach the gospel of organic gardening to the exclusion of all else. Indeed, it may come to that in a generation or so. Inorganic fertilizers, where they occur as natural deposits, are rapidly becoming exhausted. This coupled with the high costs of manufacturing them, makes 'inorganics' very expensive. In the foreseeable future we may have to rely on organic fertilizers alone but, in the meantime, I see no reason for not using 'inorganics' as additional booster feeds.

The composition of fertilizers

It is now time to dwell on the essential elements that are contained in fertilizers and that are vital to plant growth. The three that play the most important part in the plant's diet are nitrogen, phosphate and potash, represented respectively by the chemical symbols N, P and K. All three occur, in naturally balanced quantities, in most organic manures. They are also available in purely inorganic forms, either as 'specifics', where only one of the elements is present, or as compound fertilizers that contain N, P and K in more or less equal proportions. Growmore is a typical and well known example of a compound, inorganic fertilizer containing 7 per cent by weight, of each of the three essential elements. To decide which fertilizer is best for our vegetables, we have to know how each contributes to a plant's development and well-being.

Nitrogen (N)

Nitrogen is the nutritional element that encourages and supports the growth of stems and leaves. Where plants, and especially vegetables, are concerned it is very important to produce the largest leaves that it is possible for the plant to grow. The reason is that green plants are able to manufacture much of their food requirements, within their leaves, by a process called photosynthesis. As the name implies, it is the synthesis of sugars and starches, using the sun's energy to combine atmospheric carbon dioxide and water. Therefore, the larger the leaf area, the more food the plant can produce for itself. Obviously, some vegetables have potentially larger leaf areas than others. Carrots have comparatively small leaves in relation to total area, whereas cabbages and lettuce are nearly all foliage. So whilst nitrogen is essential to all vegetables it is of even greater utility to leafy crops.

Armed with this knowledge you can increase the yield of all vegetables, and of large-leaved crops in particular, by adding extra nitrogen where and when it will do most good.

Experimental work done at The National Vegetable Research Station, Wellesbourne, Warwickshire, has shown that a nitrogenous fertilizer applied about 10 to 14 days before sowing and planting, will increase the yield of leafy vegetables by between 20 and 50 per cent, depending on the rate of application up to a maximum of 225 grams (8 oz) per square metre of a 10 per cent N fertilizer. Another characteristic of nitrogen is that it is highly soluble in all its fertilizer forms. As a result, there are no residual nitrogen salts left in the soil after one season of growth and rain. Any that are not used by the plants are washed out by rainfall. It is, therefore, absolutely necessary to replace the nitrogen every year shortly before sowing and planting.

A nitrogen shortage in the soil is unmistakable. The plants are stunted and their leaves, besides being undersized, are yellowish-green with sometimes a reddish discoloration.

Sources of nitrogen as a fertilizer:

Organic sources	*% N*	*Inorganic sources*	*% N*
Cow manure	0.6	Sulphate of ammonia	21.0
Horse manure	0.7	Nitrate of soda	16.0
Pig manure	0.5	Nitro-chalk	21.0
Chicken manure	1.1	Nitrate of potash	13.0
Mushroom compost	0.8	Growmore	7.0
Garden compost	0.7		
Bone meal*	3.2		
Boneflour*	1.2		
Dried blood*	13.0		
Fish meal*	9.5		
Hoof and horn*	13.0		

* Denotes concentrated, derived organic fertilizers.

Manures and mushroom and garden composts vary in their fertilizer value and the above percentages should be taken as averages.

A feature of organic fertilizers in general is that, as their nitrogen is released slowly into the soil, heavy applications are unlikely to damage plants. The exception is fresh poultry manure, which contains some nitrogen as free ammonia and this can harm the roots. If it is fresh, poultry manure should be left for several weeks in the open to get rid of the excess ammonia. Overdoses of inorganic nitrogen are exceedingly damaging, due to its high solubility. Always stick to the recommended rates of application on the fertilizer packs and apply them to growing plants only when the soil is nicely moist. Also make sure that no fertilizer crystals or granules fall on the leaves to cause severe scorching.

Phosphate (P)

Phosphate does its work below soil level. It is the nutritional element that contributes to root development. Roots have two functions to perform in the lives of plants. They provide them with a firm anchorage and they enable them to absorb water and plant food in solution. Therefore, a good fibrous root system gives plants a firm foothold on the threshold of life.

In the vegetable plot, phosphate is essential to everything we grow and is especially needed by root crops, such as carrots, beetroot, parsnips and others. All these vegetables develop swollen tap-roots for the purpose of food storage and it is these roots that we eat fresh and store for winter use. A little extra phosphate applied to these crops will increase their yield. However, phosphates are a lot less soluble than nitrates and a percentage is carried over in the soil from one season to the next. Therefore, on soils that are regularly maintained in a fertile state, by the use of organic fertilizers, it should be sufficient to apply 56 grams (2 oz) of superphosphate per square metre to the root crop area only.

Sources of phosphate as a fertilizer:

Organic sources	*% P*	*Inorganic sources*	*% P*
Cow manure	0.2	Superphosphate	20.0
Pig manure	0.3	Triple superphosphate	47.0
Horse manure	0.3	Growmore	7.0
Chicken manure	0.8		
Mushroom compost	0.6		
Garden compost	0.2		
Bone meal*	29.0		
Boneflour*	29.0		
Hoof and horn*	2.0		
Fish meal*	10.0		

* Denotes concentrated, derived organic fertilizers.

Where the soil is deficient in phosphate, plants will develop poor root systems, with a consequent substandard growth of leaves and stems.

Potash (K)

Potash does not contribute directly to the growth of plants. What is does is to give them full functional efficiency. Where there is a potash deficiency, there is an increased danger of various fungal diseases occurring, whereas an adequate potash level gives plants an inbuilt disease resistance. Potash also assists ripening as plants approach maturity. It is, therefore, of signal importance to fruit crops such as tomatoes, cucumbers, peppers, marrows and legumes and also to onions and shallots when their bulbs begin to swell.

As with phosphates, there is usually a residual quantity of potash remaining in the soil, from season to season, where a comprehensive fertility programme has been followed. Vegetable plots that are regularly manured should not need more than 225 grams (8 oz) of a specific potash fertilizer per square metre, per annum.

Sources of potash as a fertilizer:

Organic sources	*% K*	*Inorganic sources*	*% K*
Cow manure	0.5	Sulphate of potash	48.0
Pig manure	0.5	Muriate of potash	60.0
Horse manure	0.6	Nitrate of potash	44.0
Chicken manure	0.5	Growmore	7.0
Mushroom compost	0.6		
Garden compost	0.4		

The first sign of a potash deficiency is a browning of the leaves around the edges. Where the deficiency is severe the 'scorching' effect may spread over the whole leaf area.

Nitrogen, phosphate and potash – these are the elements essential to strong, healthy plant growth. They may be added to the soil in either their organic or inorganic forms, or by combining both. Whichever method is used, it is of vital importance to apply the relevant fertilizer at the time of year when it will be most beneficial. Fresh manures take a long time to decompose and release their nutritional elements and they should be dug in in the autumn and early winter. Soil bacteria will work on them during the winter months, and by spring their plant foods will be readily available to the plants.

Concentrated and composted organic fertilizers break down more rapidly and need not be dug in until January or early February. Being highly soluble, inorganic fertilizers would be wasted if they were dug in, in autumn or winter. By the time the plant roots were ready to receive them, a fair amount of their goodness would have been washed down, out of their reach. The best time to add the inorganics is about two weeks before sowing and planting and they should be forked into the top 5 or 6 cm, rather than be turned in with a spade.

My feeding plan

In my own vegetable plot I concentrate on maximum production, striving to get as much out of the limited area of ground as I possibly can. My close-cropping plan calls for high soil fertility that I achieve by digging in large quantities of well-rotted manure and compost in January, followed by a forked-in dressing of 'Blood, Fish and Bone' fertilizer at 4 oz to the square yard in early March. The 'Blood, Fish and Bone' is a ready-mixed fertilizer compounded from dried blood, fish meal and bone meal. It is rich in nitrogen and phosphate, but virtually devoid of potash. To make sure that my vegetables do not go short of potash, I give them a liquid feed of high potash fertilizer in May; twice, at two-week intervals. This simple feeding programme yields a bountiful crop of good, healthy vegetables at comparatively low cost.

I have mentioned the liquid feeding of outdoor crops. In reality I regard liquid fertilizers as being of prime importance only in the greenhouse and on vegetables grown in containers, either indoors or out. Their value in the vegetable plot is secondary to the major, solid fertilizers applied before sowing and planting and they should be regarded as booster feeds only. The main asset of liquid fertilizers lies in the accessibility of their plant foods. Being already in solution, their N.P.K. elements are absorbed by plants immediately following application. Furthermore, the elements are taken into the plants' life stream through the leaves as well as through the roots. This being so, plants respond very rapidly to an overhead watering of liquid fertilizer at the recommended dilution. Therefore, if you have a patch of vegetables that appear to be lagging behind, water them with a liquid fertilizer, such as Phostrogen, and they will quickly take on a new and healthier look.

Trace elements

It is up to every individual gardener to decide in what form he will apply N, P and K. If he is wise he will concentrate on the organic, bulky manures to keep his soil lively and fundamentally fertile. In addition, he may use inorganic fertilizers as supplementary feeds. If he follows these basic principles is he doing enough? At this point I draw a comparison between plants and humans. Our main diet consists of proteins, carbohydrates and fats. As with the N, P and K in plant life, our dietary constituents, consumed in balanced amounts, build healthy bodies and maintain them in good condition. But, as every dietician knows, we also need small quantities of vitamins to achieve peak fitness; without them our susceptibility to disease is increased. Similarly plants need minute amounts of 'trace elements' for the same reasons. They are well named because only traces of them are needed, yet if they are totally absent plants will develop deficiency symptoms. A total lack of magnesium, or iron, results in yellowish leaves; and a deficiency of boron is expressed in heart-rot in certain root crops such as the beet family. Other trace elements include, zinc, molybdenum, iodine and manganese. Trace element deficiency is uncommon and rarely, if ever, occurs in soils that are regularly dressed with organic manures. Gardeners who rely solely on inorganic fertilizers may find their soils short of magnesium and/or iron, the trace element deficiencies that are most likely to be a problem. Should they occur they can be quickly put right by watering the crops with a solution of a dessertspoonful of Epsom salts in 9 litres (2 gallons) of water to replace the lost magnesium and a similar dilution of alum to restore the iron level. In the rare event of boron deficiency apply 28 grams (1 oz) of borax to every 40 sq. metres (50 sq. yd) of soil area.

The importance of lime

The one remaining nutritional element required by plants is calcium in the form of lime. It is not as vital as N, P and K, yet it is more, much more, than a trace element.

Lime has many parts to play in the drama of plant growth. To begin with it has the power to make heavy, clay soils lighter by a process known as flocculation. It breaks clay up and keeps it from becoming an impermeable 'rice-pudding' in winter and a hard-packed, cracked surface in summer. On such a soil you can apply heavy dressings of lime; anything up to 225 grams (8 oz) to the square metre will do a world of good. But never apply lime at the same time as any other organic or inorganic fertilizer. If you do, the one will neutralize the other and the beneficial effects of both will be lost. Leave at least three months between dressings of lime and applications of N.P.K. fertilizers. Being alkaline, lime also 'sweetens' the soil. Most fertilizers are of an acidic nature and their repeated application can result in the soil becoming excessively acid or 'sour'. Lime corrects the over-acidity. Lastly, certain crops have a pronounced liking for the calcium element in lime, whilst others are better off without it. Root crops do not need lime and this applies especially to potatoes. In freshly limed ground potatoes develop scabs and whilst the crop remains edible, its keeping qualities are greatly impaired. The one crop group that revels on lime-treated ground is the cabbage family – the brassicas. They need the calcium and they are less prone to club root attack if lime is present (*see also* Chapter 7). The answer to how, when and where to lime is to apply it only when needed, and annually to the brassica patch; which leads me to crop rotation.

Crop rotation

Crop rotation involves placing our vegetables into groups and then growing the groups in different parts of the vegetable plot in successive years. For our purposes three groups are sufficient, as follows:

Group 1: the brassicas; namely, cabbage, cauliflower, Brussels sprouts, broccoli and kale and including swedes and turnips. Surprising as it may seem, swedes and turnips belong to the same plant family (the *Cruciferae*) as brassicas, and they are, therefore, similarly affected by external influences.

Group 2: this includes all members of the legume family – the pulses, peas, broad beans, runner beans, dwarf french beans, pole beans and others.

Group 3: into this group go the remaining root crops such as beetroot, carrots and parsnips, the salad vegetables and anything else that has no place in Groups 1 and 2.

A THREE-YEAR CROP ROTATION			
	Plot area A	**Plot area B**	**Plot area C**
1st year	peas and beans	brassicas, swedes and turnips	root crops, salads and others
2nd year	brassicas, swedes and turnips	root crops, salads and others	peas and beans
3rd year	root crops, salads and others	peas and beans	brassicas, swedes and turnips

There are two very good reasons why every gardener should operate a simple three-year crop rotation system. Firstly, different crops use up different amounts of nitrogen, phosphate and potash. Residual fertilizers left by one crop will be used to advantage by another crop group, grown in the same ground the following year. In addition, the legume family possesses an ability peculiar to itself alone. Roots of peas and beans are dotted with small swellings, or nodules, that can assimilate nitrogen from the air and convert into nitrogenous fertilizer. Therefore, a non-leguminous crop, following peas and beans, will find a ready-made supply of nitrogen at its roots.

Secondly, all members of a particular vegetable family are susceptible to the attentions of certain insect pests and diseases. For example, the cabbage root fly will pounce on all brassicas, swedes and turnips, but will ignore all other vegetables. Just as there are horses for courses, so there are pests for pulses and other vegetable families. It is also known that both insects and fungus diseases can lie inactive in the soil over winter. In spring they again become active and renew their attacks on the host plants. As a result, the same vegetable groups, grown each year in the same patch, become more and more pest-ridden as the pest population increases. By moving the groups around the plot, there is less likelihood of a pest build-up and therefore the plants are, to some degree, safeguarded from attack. Finally, by working a three-year crop rotation and applying lime to the brassica group only, this is equivalent to liming the whole plot once every three years and keeping the soil sweet.

SOIL TYPES

Having dwelt on the origins of soil and its fertility, it is time to recognize that not all soils are similar. They vary considerably in their structure and texture from country to country, even from county to county and from garden to garden in some areas. The only thing they all have in common is their need for the essential plant foods. Yet this common denominator is itself variable, as different soil types possess different retentive powers. In Britain as a whole, soils come in three main categories – sand, clay and loam, with peat- and chalk-based soils occurring only in a few localities.

Sandy soils

I once had a garden on a soil that was pure sand of an indeterminate depth. I recall workmen from the Electricity Board arriving to dig a hole for a new pylon in the adjoining field. They dug down a full 4 metres without reaching subsoil. It was sand from top to bottom, with the top foot depth a darker colour than the remaining 15 feet. I blessed and cursed that soil. Digging it was as easy as slicing butter. The spade sank up to its hilt, using hand pressure alone and came up laden, as light as a midsummer morning. There its blessings ended. To grow anything to a reasonable standard, I had to pour in tonne after tonne of organic manure, supplemented by many kilos of concentrated fertilizers. Given this generous treatment, it grew carrots and parsnips that would have taken the red card at any show in the country. But being a man of limited means I soon moved house.

The trouble with a sandy soil is its insatiable appetite for fertilizers. It is composed of large, hard particles that have little ability to retain plant nutrients. Liquids of all kinds, including water and soluble plant foods pass through it easily and quickly. It is, therefore, a hungry soil and one that dries out rapidly during dry spells. The only way to improve it is to apply as much manure or garden compost as you can spare, every year. Its humus content will gradually increase in the long term, but it will always need constant bulk feeding, followed by 'concentrates'. It will also need copious watering in dry weather. Because of its porous nature, a sandy soil is one on which it might be advisable to practise the no-digging method of cultivation. Instead of digging in manure, apply really well-rotted organic material, on the surface, a month or two before sowing and planting time. In this way the manure's goodness will leach down gradually into the topsoil and less will be wasted. Also, the soil structure will not be disturbed. It will become more compact and, in consequence, more retentive.

Clay soils

I have also gardened on a clay soil and broken a spade and very nearly my back. A clay soil is as heavy as lead and almost as impermeable to water. It is composed of very small particles that cling together to form a solid block. On the credit side, a clay soil retains moisture and nutrients, and, with patience, understanding and much sweat, it can be converted to a good, workable and fertile soil.

To conquer clay I suggest the following, annual plan of campaign. When the ground is vacant in the autumn, dig it with a fork and after digging top dress with 225 grams (8 oz) of lime to the square metre. Leave it rough to let the lime and frost break down the hard, unyielding lumps. In January, trench the whole area to a depth of 30 cm (1 ft) and line the trenches with plenty of manure or compost before closing them in. The combined flocculating action of the lime and the humus-forming action of the organics, will steadily change the light-coloured hard clay to a nice, dark, rich and crumbly soil. I know, because it took me a mere five years to effect the transformation.

Loam soils

The gardener on loam is either wise or lucky. If he is wise he would have examined the soil before deciding to build, or buy, his house on it. If he is just lucky he should take full advantage of his good fortune and grow the kind of vegetables that are the envy of his sandy-soiled neighbour.

A loam is dark in colour, rich in humus and easy to cultivate. Because of its high humus content, it holds moisture and nutrients and releases them gradually, as and when they are needed by the growing plants. Given such a valuable asset, it is our responsibility as gardeners to maintain the soil's fertility level by the methods previously described in this chapter.

There has always been much argument and debate as to whether a good loam should be dug or left undug. The no-digging exponents maintain that digging upsets the soil structure to the detriment of plant growth. Advocates of digging claim that it aerates the soil, puts the fertilizers where they are needed, where the plant roots will be and that it gives better weed control. I believe both schools of thought have merit – it just depends when the digging is done. If it is done in the autumn and early winter, the soil has plenty of time to settle down and to re-establish its structure. But if digging is left until a few short weeks before sowing and planting, the soil structure may well be too open and lacking in consolidation. The moral, on a loamy soil is – dig early or not at all.

Chalky soils

Chalky soils predominate in some parts of Britain and usually consist of an alkaline topsoil overlying a subsoil of limestone, or chalk. Soils of this nature do not need liming, but they do require generous dressings of organic manure, to counteract the high alkalinity and to maintain good fertility. In wet weather chalk-based soils become tacky and unworkable, but they drain quickly. In common with sandy soils, they need to be kept watered during dry spells in the growing season.

Peaty soils

Peaty soils occur infrequently and are of two types. Fen peats possess the potential for high fertility, that, once achieved, is easily sustained. Acid peats on the other hand are badly drained and acutely short of lime and plant foods. They can be reclaimed to a reasonable level of fertility by draining, applying carbonate of lime annually at between 225 to 340 grams (8 to 12 oz) to the square metre and top dressing with a general, concentrated fertilizer at around 56 grams (2 oz) per square metre. Their high acidity will take several years before it will approach neutrality (pH 7.0) and during this period of correction the only crop likely to do reasonably well are potatoes.

These are the soil types that you may encounter in your gardening life. They all have the potential to be highly fertile and productive, some more so than others. But, whatever the basic composition of your soil, I stress again that it is only by providing your vegetables with an ample supply of balanced plant foods in the presence of a high level of humus that true fertility can be attained and maintained.

Cultivating the soil

There are two equally convincing schools of thought on the subject of soil cultivation – the no-diggers and the diggers. The no-diggers expound on the merits of leaving the soil undisturbed, so that its granular structure remains constant and in its natural state. They apply their organic and inorganic fertilizers on the surface and leave it to the weather, earthworms and other soil animals to take them down to the plant roots. The diggers maintain that the soil must be dug to aerate it and that in the process they can incorporate fertilizers into the lower reaches of the top soil, where the roots can find them. I believe that both schools have validity.

On light and very light soils aeration is always good, because they do not compact too solidly under constant treading. Therefore the no-digging principle works. Medium to heavy soils, however, will compact under heavy feet and they will surely benefit from being turned over and aired. Provided the digging is done in the autumn, as soon as the ground is clear of crops, the soil will have plenty of time to settle and to re-establish its structure before sowing and planting begins in spring. In addition, the organic manures that are dug in at the same time are given a sufficiently long period to decompose into available plant foods, before the plants begin looking for them some months later. In other words, know your soil type and cultivate it accordingly.

How deep?

The second big question is – how deeply should the soil be dug? In the days when labour was cheap and time was less pressing, many gardeners were addicted to the torture of 'double-digging', or 'bastard-trenching' as it was also called. This involved digging a series of trenches, removing the top 30 cm (1 ft) of soil, or spit and digging manure into the bottom 30 cm (1 ft) in the trench, before replacing the top spit – a spit being defined as the depth of a spade. It is a slow and tedious process that can prove highly beneficial on a heavy, badly drained soil. Double-digging also increases the depth of fertility, as the subsoil is gradually brought to life by the organic manure, with its nutrients and active bacteria. But on reasonably good soils, that drain easily, double digging is a waste of time and effort, with possibly a few exceptions. For deep-rooting vegetables, such as runner beans, it is worth taking out a 40-cm (2-ft) deep trench. Most vegetables, though, are shallow rooters and, providing the soil drains well, single-spit digging is adequate.

Easy does it!

The purpose of turning over the top spit of soil is to aerate it, to freshen it up after much of it has been compacted by treading during the season of growth. The first lesson is – never dig when the soil is wet and sticks to your footwear. A sodden soil is heavy and makes for hard labour. The second lesson is to tackle the job in the right frame of mind. Don't go out with the intention of completing the job in the shortest possible time. Rather, treat the operation as a pleasant interlude from the tedium of everyday life and do a bit at a time. If your plot is 12 metres (40 ft) wide, divide it roughly into four 3-metre

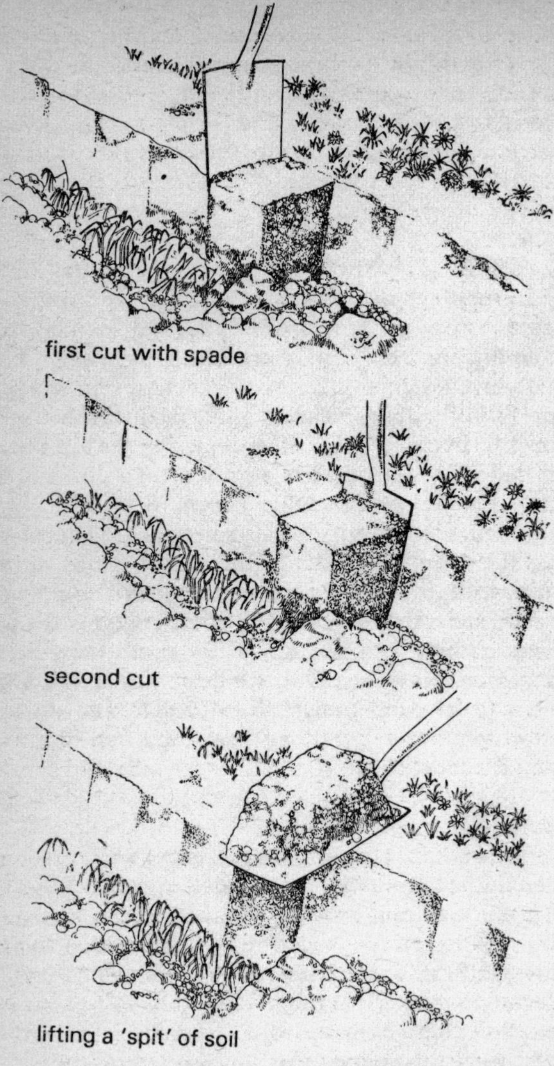

Single digging

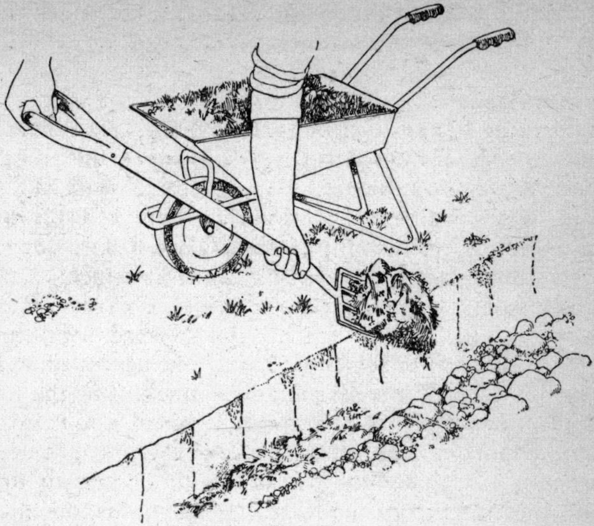

Spreading manure in a trench

(10-ft) wide strips and dig a strip at a time. Digging it piecemeal is a great morale booster, for the simple reason that there are four ends to achieve and each one is completed fairly quickly. Also take small bites at the soil rather than big ones. Until you find your digging rhythm, a clod of soil the width of the spade and about 10 cm (4 in.) deep will be enough to handle. As your back and shoulders get used to the task and a natural rhythm is established, you will find you can turn larger clods fairly effortlessly.

So, let us begin. Dig out a trench 30 cm (1 ft) deep at the top end of the strip, put the soil in a wheelbarrow, trundle it to the bottom end and leave it there. To lift a clod of soil, first put the spade in at a right angle to the trench, then thrust it in a second time at a right angle to the first cut. Lever the clod upwards and turn it and throw it forward into the trench, in one movement. If you are adding manure at the same time, put it into the trench before you throw the soil forward. Proceed in this way down the strip until you reach the bottom, when you end up with a trench which you fill from the barrowload of soil taken out at the start of the proceedings. It is simple, providing it is done in a relaxed, easy manner.

Green manuring

The digging I have described relates to soil that is devoid of plant growth. If the soil is covered in weeds the procedure varies very slightly. Before filling each trench with soil, skim off the weeds with the spade and turn them, soil side uppermost, into the bottom of the trench. They will rot down and convert into plant foods. In fact, some gardeners regularly practise what is termed 'green manuring'. This entails sowing a crop of something like agricultural mustard or rape in the autumn, as soon as the crops have been harvested and the ground is bare. The seeds germinate quickly and the crop is dug in when the plants are about 22 to 30 cm (9 to 12 in.) tall. After digging in, the green manure rots slowly, releasing nitrogen, phosphates and potash into the soil, ready for the following year's crops and increasing its humus content.

A grass site

Finally, there is the question of starting a vegetable patch on a lawn, or from an area of pasture. In neither case is it advisable to dig the turf into the soil. Turf invariably holds a high population of grass and weed seeds, and, in pastureland, it also has a fair number of growing annual and perennial weeds. The best course is cut the turf into 30-cm (1-ft) squares, lift the turves with about 2 cm (1 in.) of soil and stack them upside down for a year or more. Given time the turves will rot down to a friable loam that is just right for use as a potting medium, or for putting back into runner bean and celery trenches.

Mulching

Mulching is a term used when a layer of decayed organic material is placed between and around plants. Peat and well-rotted manure and garden compost make ideal mulching materials. A mulch placed between rows of vegetables helps to control weeds by smothering them and it helps to keep the soil temperature fairly constant by preventing excessive loss of warmth during cold weather. A mulch also keeps the soil nicely moist by reducing the volume of water loss by evaporation from the surface.

Water is as vital to vegetables as are plant foods. Without it they cannot absorb nutrients in solution, neither can they remain turgid and in growth. Long before they reach wilting point in an inadequately moist soil, plants will cease growing and suffer a severe check from which they may never fully recover. In dry spells as much as two to three gallons of water per square yard may be needed by rapidly growing vegetables. It is not enough just to 'show them the can'; they need a sprinkler left running until the ground is thoroughly saturated. By reducing water loss, mulching lessens the need for constant watering and the crops are better for the more regulated water level at their roots.

During growth, regular use of the hoe is an essential part of soil cultivation. A few minutes spent hoeing between the rows each week, demolishes the weeds as they come through and keeps the soil surface open so that water and air can flow freely through it.

4

SOWING AND PLANTING

Growing vegetables from seeds rather than buying in young plants is not only the most interesting and rewarding way, it is also the most economical. After many years of gardening I still experience the same creative thrill of waiting for the first spring-sown seeds to germinate. Seeing them coming through is a kind of guarantee that Nature's cycle will remain unbroken and that life will go on.

The quality and potential of vegetable seeds packed and sold in Britain are high. Indeed, they are all subject to certain stringent standards, as stipulated by E.E.C. regulations, in respect of their purity and germination. Therefore, the seeds you buy can be confidently expected to germinate, providing you help them by providing them with the right conditions. If they do not germinate, you may be sure that one or more of these conditions have not been met.

Moisture

Seeds represent life in a state of deep dormancy. Fundamentally, they consist of either one or two starch storage organs (cotyledons) encased in a seed coat of varying thickness, together with an inert growing point called the hilum. Usually the hilum rests beneath a protective tissue, that is seen on most seeds as a scar. It is from the hilum that the young root and shoot spring to life, relying on the starchy food stored in the cotyledons to sustain growth until the first leaves open and the seedling becomes self-sufficient. For the seed to break its dormancy there must be moisture in the soil, to penetrate the seed coat and cause the cotyledons to swell and soften. In a totally dry soil, seeds will remain inert until they perish from old age.

Air

Most living things need air as part of their life-support systems and germinating seeds are no exception. In a well cultivated soil, with a friable surface, an adequate air supply is no problem. The only soil type that is likely to be poorly ventilated is a heavy, consolidated clay, where the soil particles lie so closely together that air is excluded. Such a soil results in poor germination and every effort is needed to improve its texture and aeration as described in Chapter 3.

Warmth

Varying degrees of warmth are vital for good germination. Below their critical minimum temperature requirements, seeds cannot germinate. In broad outline, these critical temperatures are related to the geographical and ancestral origins of the present-day vegetable varieties grown in our gardens. Seeds of plants that are natural natives of cold to cool climates will germinate successfully at soil temperatures in the region of 5.5°C (40°F). In contrast, seeds of sub-tropical and tropical species need germination temperatures in a range from 15°C to 20°C (60°F to 70°F). In our temperate British climate the variation in temperature requirements for germination leads to a convenient and general classification of plants into hardy and half-hardy groups.

Hardy vegetables

The leading group includes most of the vegetables we grow, e.g. onions, leeks, carrots, broad beans, lettuces and so on. Being hardy their seeds are sown directly into the open ground as soon as the soil temperature is sufficiently high to support germination. Regrettably, there is no magical date to indicate when the temperature is right. Sowing time outdoors is as variable as the weather. In a mild, early spring in the South you may sow successfully in early March, whereas after an ice-cold winter and a reluctant spring, in the same area, sowing may have to be delayed until well into April. The best advice passed on to me long ago by an aged gardener is 'wait until you see the weeds begin to grow'. Then you know that Nature is ready for rebirth and you can put your seeds in. I have followed his wisdom and it never fails. This rule applies to practically all the hardy vegetables normally sown outdoors, with the exception of beetroot, runner beans and dwarf French beans. They need a slightly higher temperature. Beetroot sowings should be delayed until late April and outdoor sowings of runner and dwarf French beans left until about the middle to the end of May, depending on locality. In Britain there is usually a temperature and growth lag of about a month between the north and south of the country.

Half-hardy vegetables

The half-hardy group includes vegetables whose seeds will only germinate successfully in spring, in some form of applied warmth. They include such things as tomatoes, peppers, aubergines, cucumbers, melons and celery. However, it does not necessarily follow that, having germinated, the young plants cannot be grown outdoors, if planting out is delayed until there is no further danger of frost.

The half-hardies require a germination temperature of between 15°C to 20°C (60°F to 70°F) and this is where gardening can become costly. The days of cheap fuel have long gone and it is now very expensive to heat a greenhouse to these temperature ranges. Fortunately, there are ways of achieving heating economy without sacrificing germination levels. One way is to sow the seeds in pots or trays, placing these in a small electrically-heated propagator. The necessary temperatures can be reached and maintained for a few pence per day. After germination the seedlings are taken out of the propagator and grown on in the greenhouse at lower temperatures. A good, thermostatically controlled propagator is fairly expensive to buy, but in terms of fuel cost economy, it is well worth the investment.

Germination on the cheap

The cheapest way of all is to sow the seeds in a plastic seed tray and then place this into a polythene bag with the open end tucked tightly under the tray. The tray is placed in a heated airing cupboard and left unattended until the seedlings appear. During germination, seeds do not need light, but the

Electrically heated propagator

moment the seedlings are through, the tray should be taken out of the plastic bag and placed where it will get maximum light, to prevent the seedlings getting thin and spindly. The plastic bag prevents water from soiling the clothing in the airing cupboard. It also prevents water loss by evaporation, so there is no need to water the seed tray until the bag is removed.

A large, home-made propagator
For gardeners who grow so many plants from seed that neither the airing cupboard, nor a standard propagator are sufficient, the answer is to convert all or part of the greenhouse staging into a massive propagator. It is quite simple. All you need is an aluminium, solid-based staging, some clean, fine grit, or Perlite, a length of soil-warming cable, lengths of 127 by 8 mm (5 by ⅜ in.) wood, sheets of fairly heavy gauge polythene and a fish-tank thermostat. The lengths of wood are cut to size and fitted on to the outer rims of the staging to form an enclosure. A

couple of centimetres of grit or Perlite is spread over the base of the staging and the soil-warming cable placed on it in a series of loops, the loops being about 15 cm (6 in.) apart at their widest point. The cable is covered with a further 1 to 2 cm (½ to 1 in.) of grit or Perlite and connected to the thermostat. Finally, the polythene sheet is tacked on to one side of the wooden frame and drawn over the enclosed staging to form a heat-retaining shroud. With the thermostat set at 18°C (65°F) a steady temperature of between 15°C to 18°C (60°F to 65°F) will prevail beneath the shroud. In the popular 2.4 × 1.8 metre (8 × 6 ft) greenhouse a home-made propagator of this type will (at the time of writing) guarantee good germination of half-hardy seeds for little more than £1 per week. It will also generate enough heat to raise the air temperature in the greenhouse by several degrees to afford total frost protection.

Sowing outdoors

When the soil is reasonably dry and doesn't stick to your footwear, it is in the right condition for sowing. Before starting, give it a final raking to remove stones, to level it off and to get the top centimetre or two of soil into a fine and friable tilth. Sowing is simple, but remember that in the interests of appearances and subsequent maintenance, it pays to sow in nicely spaced, straight rows. Distances between rows are related to the size of the vegetables being grown at maturity. Swedes, being large, need to be 45 to 60 cm (1½ to 2 ft) apart all round, while carrots can be grown in rows only 15 to 22 cm (6 to 9 in.) apart. If in doubt, consult the backs of your seed packets, where the information is clearly given. These recommended distances between rows assume a soil of average fertility. On a highly fertile soil, the distances may be reduced by as much as a third, or a half; the richer the soil the more vegetable growth it will support.

Tools for the job

For seed sowing outdoors you need only four tools – a spade to sow peas and beans; a draw hoe to sow small seeds; a garden line tied to two stout pegs, and a rake. Decide on the position of your first row, place one line peg firmly in position, walk to the

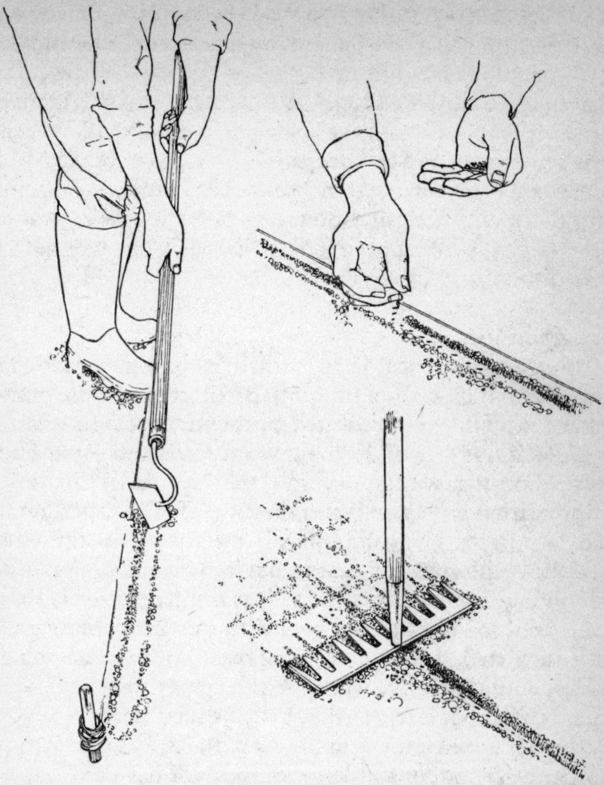

Sowing seeds outdoors

other end of the plot and loosely position the second peg. Rotate the second peg until the line is as tight as a violin string and push the peg into the soil, up to its hilt. Take the draw hoe in your hands and, starting at one end, place the blade against the line at an angle of 45 degrees. Then, with its tip in the soil, walk backwards drawing out a shallow furrow, or drill, as you go. Keep your back foot on the line to prevent it bellying out under the pressure of the hoe blade. Before sowing the open drill, move the line to the next drill position, then sow thinly in the first drill and use the rake to close it. Finish off by patting the soil down with the back of the rake to bring soil and seed into close contact. Move on and sow the second row and keep going until the job is finished.

Peas and beans need slightly different treatment. Again put the line down, and, with the spade, take out a shallow trench about 2 to 4 cm (1 to 2 in.) deep and about 30 cm (12 in.) wide. The seeds are sown in the trench at the recommended spacings. Cover them with soil, firm down, and, in the case of peas and runner beans, place supports (such as twigs, canes or netting) in position.

Sowing indoors

Prior to the mid-1930s, indoor sowings were generally made into wooden boxes containing sifted soil from a fertile place in the garden. The soil presented problems, because it always contained a number of dormant weed seeds and sometimes a variety of pests as well. As a result, the sown seeds germinated in competition with weeds and they were liable to pest attack. In the late 1930s The John Innes Horticultural Institute published the results on their researches into formulating the ideal seed sowing compost. It consisted, as it still does, of a mixture of sterilized loam, sand and peat with a quantity of fertilizer. Being sterilized, John Innes composts, both for sowing and potting, contain no live weed seeds or pests and the fertilizer ensures the good, strong growth of the seedlings.

A further development in the early 1960s was the introduction of peat-based, or soil-less, composts. They are composed of high-grade, granulated peat, again with added fertilizers and trace elements. Both types of compost are excellent and I strongly advocate their use for indoor seed sowings.

Today, plastic seed trays have largely superseded wooden ones. They are more permanent and are not so liable to harbour fungal pests. To sow, fill the seed tray with compost, to within 1 cm (½ in.) of its rim and scatter the seeds thinly on the surface. Cover them with just enough compost to hide them from view and gently firm the surface before giving them a soaking with water. Remember to stick a label in the tray to identify the contents.

On average, seedlings will appear in about two to three

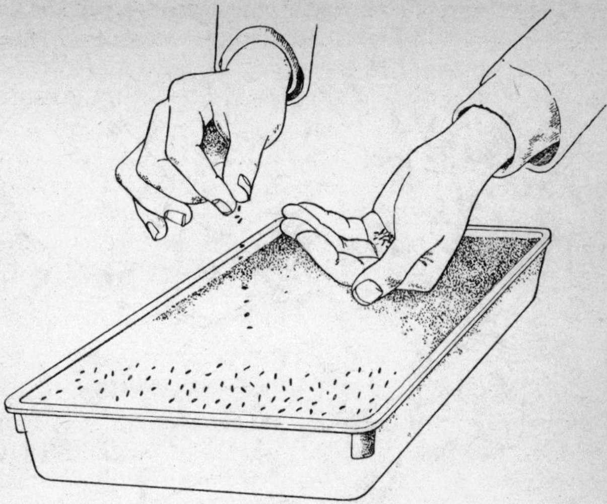

Seed sowing in a tray of compost

weeks' time. The germination period varies according to the type of seed sown and to the temperature. The first leaves to unfold are the cotyledon leaves, that usually bear little resemblance to the true leaves that follow. Keep the compost moist and avoid overwatering. The only trouble that the seedlings may meet in their young lives is a fungus disease called 'damping-off'. It attacks them at soil level causing them to keel over and die. The disease is a symptom of over-watering, of a still and humid atmosphere and of the seedlings being overcrowded. Therefore, always sow thinly, try to keep the atmosphere fresh and buoyant and use Cheshunt Compound as a preventive and curative measure.

When the seedlings have grown their first pair of true leaves they are ready for 'pricking out'. This entails uprooting and transplanting them 5 cm (2 in.) apart in trays, or singly in 75-cm (3-in.) pots, filled with a suitable potting compost. The job has to be done carefully to avoid damaging the tender seedlings. Push a dibber (or an ordinary pencil) into the compost

Pricking out seedlings

near the seedlings and very gently lever them up, taking care not to break the tiny roots. When the roots are free, take one leaf between finger and thumb and transfer the seedlings individually to their holes in the waiting tray or pot. Gently firm them in, water them and leave them to grow into robust plants for planting out in due season. In the case of seeds that are large enough to be handled individually, it is worth sowing them singly in 75-cm (3-in.) pots of potting compost. This does away with the need for pricking-out so the seedlings are not subjected to a root check. Plants like tomatoes, cucumbers and marrows lend themselves to direct sowing.

Thinning outdoor sowings

Seedlings from outdoor sowings also need thinning to give them room to develop naturally. I like to thin them as soon as I can easily get hold of them. The smaller the seedlings are, the less they feel the effects of root disturbance. Try to do the job when the soil is moist and thin out to the distances apart advised in the table on p. 19. With thinning completed, draw a little soil up on each side of the row to support the remaining seedlings that have now lost the support of their neighbours. Seedlings that have been removed with care and with their roots intact may be replanted to fill gaps in the rows.

The seed bed

Every vegetable garden needs a seed bed. It need not be large, but it is essential. Mine measures 1.8 metres (6 ft) in width by 3 metres (10 ft) in length and in it are sown those vegetables that need temporary quarters before being planted out in their final position. Its main function is as a staging post for vegetables such as leeks, cabbages, Brussels sprouts, purple sprouting broccoli, calabrese, kale and hearting broccoli, and, of course, for biennial and perennial flowers. Most of the vegetables just mentioned are follow-on crops. For example, winter cabbages are sown in the seed bed in April and later transplanted into ground vacated by summer crops such as broad beans or early potatoes.

Pelleted seeds

Pelleted seeds are small seeds that have been encased in an inert material for the express purpose of making them large enough to be handled individually. When making outdoor sowings, I place the pellets in the drills at half the spacing recommended for the mature plants. This is a safeguard against failures. It is a simple matter to pull out unwanted plants after germination. In other words, if the recommended thinning distance is 30 cm (12 in.) apart, I sow the pellets 15 cm (6 in.) apart and later remove every other seedling, if they all come up.

For indoor sowings pellets save a lot of time and they speed growth. They may be spaced out 5 cm (2 in.) apart in the seed trays, thus eliminating the necessity for pricking out. But if you are using pelleted seeds, either indoors or out, you have to take special care that the soil, or compost, never dries out before the seedlings break through the casing. If it does dry out the casing material becomes rock hard and it will not allow water to penetrate, resulting in poor germination.

F_1 hybrid seeds

Plant breeders are currently concentrating on producing more and more F_1 hybrid vegetable varieties, because of the inherent assets they all possess. Their major characteristic is their hybrid vigour, resulting in bigger and better vegetables that are also better able to withstand the onslaughts of pests and diseases. In its simplest terms an F_1 hybrid is a first generation cross, resulting from the marriage of two selected parents. It is the plant breeder's hope that the hybrid will possess desirable characteristics derived from both its parents. For example, one parent may have been chosen for its cropping ability and the second for its early maturing, leading (in the small percentage of such crosses which are successful) to an offspring which obligingly yields an early, heavy crop. F_1 hybrid seeds are invariably more expensive than ordinary seeds and they always will be. The reason is that seeds saved from F_1 hybrids themselves will not breed true. Therefore, a controlled cross between the two parental types has to be made afresh every year, at considerable cost to the grower. However, taking all their valuable attributes into consideration, F_1 hybrid seeds are worth every penny of the extra cost.

Sowing and planting for continuity

I aim to show how a plot can provide an all-the-year-round supply of vegetables without artificial aids such as a greenhouse, frames and cloches. By making the best possible use of available ground and by sowing the right quantities of vegetables at the right time, this objective is within every gardener's reach. The mistake that many gardeners make is to believe that all vegetables should be sown at the same time to fill the plot from end to end. Having done so they proudly inform their friends that they have 'done the garden' and infer that it can now fend for itself until next year. I have seen small back gardens so chock-full of lettuce that the occupants are fed up to the teeth with salads for every meal. I have even known gardeners grow a row of parsnips although, on their own admission, not one member of the family liked them. In such gardens there is a short summer glut of some vegetables and a scarcity of others.

Successional sowing

Our plan must be the provision of a sufficient supply of the vegetables the family enjoy, for as long a period as possible. Again taking lettuce as an example, a single 3- to 4-metre (12- to 15-ft) row is ample for the average family, but the whole row is not sown all at once. Begin by sowing a third of the row, wait until the seedlings have grown four leaves and then sow another third of the row and so on. Each part-row will provide a succession of crisp lettuce in peak condition and a glut will be avoided. Successional sowings may also be made of vegetables that are either used fresh from the ground or from store, beetroot being a typical example. Large beetroots tend to coarsen, whereas those no bigger than a golf ball are sweet and succulent. Therefore, for summer consumption, I sow a row in April, and, for storing for winter use, another couple of rows in late May or June. I treat carrots in the same way.

The term successional sowing may also refer to the sowing of different varieties of the same vegetable in order to achieve different maturity dates. For example, some cabbage varieties mature in spring, others in summer and autumn and yet others in winter. By choosing the appropriate sorts and sowing them at the right times, it is possible to cut cabbages during practically the 12 months of the year (*see* the sowing chart on page 72).

Catch cropping

Catch cropping involves growing a quick-maturing crop, harvesting it and growing a second crop on the same piece of ground. A row of radish, for example, could be followed by a row of lettuces or spinach, and a row of early peas by one of winter cabbages. Growing two or more crops in the same soil in quick succession exerts a heavy toll on plant foods. It is, therefore, essential to apply a general fertilizer as soon as the first crop is out of the ground and before sowing (or planting) the second.

Inter-cropping

Inter-cropping also demands a highly fertile soil. It means growing an early-maturing vegetable between rows of other vegetables that take longer to reach maturity. The early cropper is ready and harvested before its growth can be adversely affected by the later crop. For example, a row of early-sown lettuce may be grown in the row between runner beans, and Brussels sprouts be planted between rows of lettuces, spinach or spring onions.

5

TWO-WAY STRETCH

The gardener who puts trust in the British climate is a fatalist. He must be prepared to put up with frost damage and disappointment without complaint. He must resign himself to gathering his crops if and when Nature permits. The realist acknowledges the caprices of our climate and takes the appropriate measures to ensure that inclement weather does not seriously affect his crops; he protects them. He beats the weather by growing many of his vegetables in greenhouses, frames, or cloches. By so doing, he saves them from ice and frost and he is able to extend their season of growth by several weeks. In other words, the use of glass or plastic protective structures enables the gardener to grow a wider range of some vegetables successfully and to achieve earlier harvests of others.

Cloches

I start with cloches because they are the least expensive to buy and because I believe they are essential pieces of equipment in our British gardens. The word cloche derives from the French, *la cloche*, meaning bell, and indeed the very first cloches were just that – glass, bell-shaped domes, that were placed over individual plants to protect, or force, them. They were heavy and cumbersome and were needed in large numbers. From this initial design were developed the modern sectional cloches, that can be linked together to cover rows of vegetables, ranging in length from 60 cm (2 ft) to infinity. The first cloches available to the British gardener followed the French use of material, namely glass. They were of two types – the 'tent' cloche and the 'barn' cloche. The tent cloche consists simply of two sheets of glass placed about 30 to 38 cm (12 to 15 in.) apart, to span a row and brought together and clipped at the top to form a continuous inverted V. Such cloches are ideal for hastening seed germination and for speeding the growth of young seedlings. However, due to its restricted air space, there is little room for the vegetable crop to grow to an appreciable size. The barn cloche affords more air space. It comprises four sheets of glass – two upright side pieces and two angled roof pieces, the whole being held together by an arrangement of clips and wires to form a miniature greenhouse-shaped structure. As they are made of glass, both types of cloche permit maximum light penetration, so that the soil warms up quickly and heat retention is good. Having positioned the cloches, end to end, to form a continuous tunnel, a pane of glass is secured across each end of the row to prevent cold air blowing through.

However, glass cloches have two drawbacks. Glass is expensive, although the horticultural grade is less dear than the domestic grade. Glass is also extremely fragile and is all-too-easily broken, either when the cloches are being moved or when working near them.

Plastic and polythene models

Having cracked more cloches than I can count, I welcomed the introduction of a variety of plastic and polythene models. The cheapest are the plastic-sheet cloches that are available either as individual units of predetermined length or as tunnels constructed of continuous polythene sheeting draped over and around a series of hoops. These cloches are all excellent. They are lightweight, easily portable and quickly assembled and crops do well under them. Their main disadvantage is their lack of durability, having, as they do, a lifespan of only two or three years. They are also likely to disappear in a strong wind, unless they are very firmly anchored.

Moulded P.V.C. cloches

Preferring more durable cloches, I have settled for the moulded P.V.C. models. They are two to three times as expensive as the polythene-sheet types, but, in the long term, I am convinced of their economy. I bought my first moulded

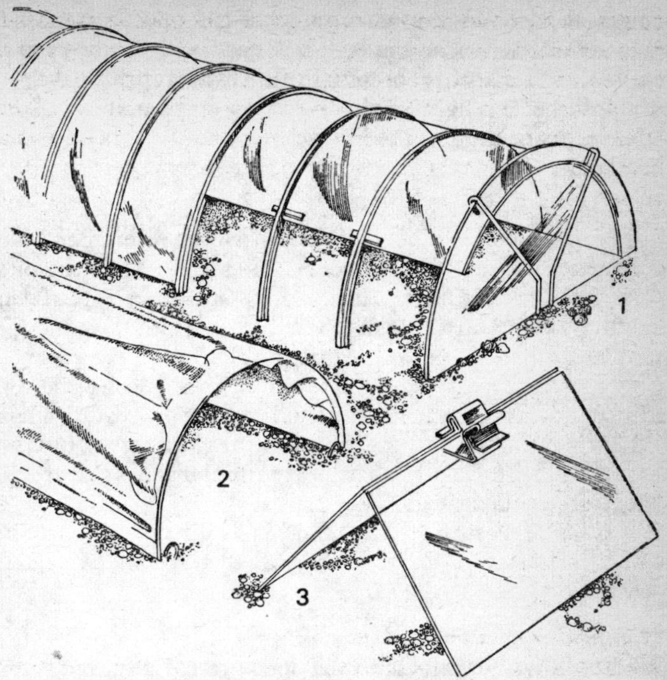

Cloches: 1 clear perspex with movable sides
2 polythene tunnel
3 glass, held by Rumsey clips

cloche eight years ago and it is still as tough, intact and efficient today as it was when new. I have even fallen over on top of it and although I inflicted slight damage to my person, the cloche remains unscathed. The type I use measures approximately 60 cm (24 in.) in length, 38 cm (15 in.) in width and 28 cm (11 in.) in height and is made of opaque plastic. The opacity reduces the danger of scorch in bright sunlight and there is good heat retention.

End-pieces for these cloches cost extra, but are essential. Being 38 cm (15 in.) wide with upright sides, the moulded P.V.C. cloche shows a further economy. I sow rows of carrots, beetroot, onions, parsnips and lettuce 22 cm (9 in.) apart, so a single cloche will cover two rows. Its 28-cm (11-in.) height also means that the cloche can be left in position until the crop is approaching maturity, or until the leaves are touching the top of the dome. It is lightweight and, in my opinion, it has all the advantages of the glass barn cloche, without its fragility and heaviness.

Other useful kinds

For large vegetable plots there is also a lot to recommend the corrugated, clear P.V.C. cloches. In essence, these are like corrugated roofing sheets, measuring some 3 metres (10 ft) in length by about 60 to 75 cm (2 to 2½ ft) in width. Wire hoops are available to shape and secure the cloches on the ground. Alternatively, the height and width of these cloches can be adjusted by using securing pegs and varying their width apart – the wider the peg spacing the wider the cloche span, but the less is its height. Finally, there are the mini-cloches that are, in effect, seed propagators. They consist of solid, moulded, clear P.V.C. and measure 60 cm (24 in.) in length, 10 cm (4 in.) in width and 88 cm (3½ in.) in height, each having two small ventilation holes on the ridge and closed ends.

Making the most of your cloches

Seeds will not germinate in the open ground until the sun's warmth has warmed the soil sufficiently. In a normal season, seeds may be sown outdoors from early March onwards, but in a late season, sowing may be delayed until well into April. By using cloches, sowing time may be advanced by as much as a month, or more.

As soon as the soil is workable in spring, I rake it level to a fine tilth, lay down the garden line and place alongside it a row of the small seed-propagating cloches, thrusting them hard down on to the soil. At this stage nothing is sown. The cloches are left in position for two weeks, to warm up the soil under the strengthening sun. They are then lifted and put to one side and the row is sown, the cloches being immediately replaced when the job is done. After germination I leave the mini-cloches in position until the seedlings are just touching the ridge, when they are moved and the young plants are thinned to their correct distances apart. After this thinning, the plants are covered over with the larger cloches to bring them along still further and faster. Using this two-cloche system, I reckon to be pulling beetroot and cutting lettuce a good two to three weeks earlier than from seeds sown without protection. The mini-cloches are also extremely useful for putting over onion sets after planting.

I also use the large moulded cloches to put over anything that appears to be dawdling and over frost-tender crops such as potatoes, marrows and sweet corn, if the need arises. They also allow me to plant out tender vegetables up to four weeks earlier than normal. For example, it is unwise to plant outdoor tomatoes before the beginning of June, unless you can give them cloche protection, and the same goes for marrows, celery, runner beans, sweet corn, ridge cucumbers and sweet peppers. With cloches to keep the cold out, all these can be put out in late April to early May. I use the same cloches later on to protect crops that would not survive the winter without them; things like rows of autumn-sown broad beans, peas and winter lettuce. For instance, I sow a row of Valdor or Arctic King lettuce in September or early October under cloches, and, by the following April, they are nicely hearted and ready for cutting. In fact, my large moulded cloches are in constant use all the year round, protecting and accelerating growth wherever they are needed. If the frame is full, I even use them to harden off tender young plants brought straight from the greenhouse. I couldn't garden without them.

The garden frame

The uses to which a garden frame can be put depend on whether or not you have a greenhouse. If you have a greenhouse a cold frame is essential for hardening-off, as I shall explain later. It also has other uses. If you have no greenhouse, a frame can be converted into a miniature greenhouse by installing soil warming cable. Basically, there are two kinds of frames; the first has wooden sides with a wooden-frame glass top, and the second is an aluminium-framed structure, with sides and top of glass. In both types the glass top either lifts or slides open and is referred to as the 'frame light'. The wood-built frame conserves warmth and is, therefore, of greater value to plants in winter than the aluminium type, which loses heat quickly through the glass and metal. The wooden frame model needs treating with a wood preservative every two or three years, whereas the aluminium structure needs no such maintenance. On balance, I prefer the wooden frame for its heat retention. Whatever type you have, give careful consideration to its siting. Ideally, the frame should be in the sunniest, most sheltered part of the garden away from cold winds and its sloping 'light' should face south to get all the available sunshine. It will also save a lot of fetching and carrying if it can be positioned right next to, or near, the greenhouse.

Frame with 'light' half open

The cold frame

My cold frame is more or less full all the year round. During the winter it houses 7-cm (3-in.) pots of autumn-sown cauliflower, lettuces and sweet peas, all of which are planted out in early spring. No sooner is it empty than it begins to fill up again with boxes and pots of half-hardy plants from the greenhouse which need to be hardened-off. These are tender plants sown and grown on in the warmth of the greenhouse and intended for outdoor planting later on – bedding plants, celery, marrows, runner beans and the like. If they were to be transferred straight from the greenhouse to the open garden, they would suffer a severe growth check due to temperature variation. So, instead of moving them direct from a greenhouse temperature range of anything from 7°C to 26°C (45°F to 80°F) to an outdoor range of about −1°C to 10°C (30°F to 50°F), they are placed in the frame to soften the blow.

During their first two or three days in the frame, the 'light' is kept closed on cold days and opened a centimetre or so on warmer, sunny days. As the plants get acclimatized, the light is propped higher and higher, until it is removed completely on warm days and replaced only at night. Even then it should be left open 2 cm on warm nights to allow for good ventilation. On really cold nights, with frost in the air, the light, even though closed right down, may not be enough to give the plants total protection. To be on the safe side, throw a few sacks on top of the light as added protection and take them off in the morning as soon as it is safe to do so. After two or three weeks of hardening-off the plants will be robust enough for planting in the open when there is no further threat of frost.

A heated frame

A cold frame can be converted into a heated frame quite easily. First put a 2-cm (1-in.) layer of grit, sand or gravel on the bottom and on it lay soil-warming cable in loops with about 10 to 15 cm (4 to 6 in.) between them. When the floor is adequately covered, continue the cable around the inside of the frame sides, forming two or three complete circuits. Then connect the cable to a suitable, insulated thermostat, itself connected to a power supply. If you doubt your ability to accomplish the job so that it is electrically sound and safe, get an electrician to do it for you. Don't run any risks, it isn't worth it. Finally, cover the base cable with 5 cm (2 in.) of grit, sand or gravel with, on top of this, about 15 cm (6 in.) of soil. A frame of this type, with under-soil and space heating, will give full frost protection for tender plants. It can also be used for very early sowings of such things as onions, leeks, cauliflowers and lettuces in boxes and for direct sowings of crops such as lettuces and radish, marrows and melons that are grown to maturity in the soil in the frame.

PLANNED SOWINGS IN A COLD FRAME		
Month to sow	**Vegetables**	**Plant out**
January	onions and leeks	April
February	radish	mature in frame
March	french beans	May-June
	carrots, beetroot, radish	mature in frame
April	french beans, runner beans, sweet corn	May-June
May	french beans, runner beans, sweet corn, marrows,	June
	frame or ridge cucumbers	mature in frame
June	salad crops	mature in frame
July		
August	winter lettuce	mature in frame
September		
October	cauliflower	March-April
November	broad beans, early peas	March
December	onions	April

The greenhouse

A greenhouse is probably the most expensive item of equipment you are likely to consider buying as a gardener. Therefore it is worthwhile pondering the pros and cons before committing yourself. For a start, resist the temptation to buy the smallest, cheapest greenhouse, simply because of its comparatively low cost. The cheapest may prove to be an unwise investment and the smallest may soon prove to be an eternal frustration. I know from experience that no matter what size greenhouse you buy, you will soon wish you had bought a bigger one. Once you begin to experience the interest and excitement of greenhouse gardening you will, like me, wish you had more room to grow a wider variety of plants. However, for the purposes of this book, I am assuming that the prime objective of a greenhouse is to grow vegetables and in particular tomatoes.

Over the years I have visited hundreds of gardens, and

almost without exception every greenhouse is chock-full of tomatoes in summer and little else. Confining oneself to a single vegetable is wasteful and boring, when so much more can be grown. In summer I like to see the greenhouse groaning under the weight of cucumbers, melons, aubergines and sweet peppers as well as tomatoes; and in winter and early spring, there are other crops to take their places. How big a 'house' do you need for this kind of production? I suggest that the bare minimum is 3.6 × 2.4 metres (12 × 8 ft) or, at a pinch, 3 × 2.4 metres (10 × 8 ft). Check the prices and you will find that a one-size larger greenhouse is not all that much more expensive than the one-size smaller model.

Which type to choose?

The next question is what kind of greenhouse should you choose? It can be wood or metal framed, half glass or all glass and of varying shapes. If I were given the choice and if my bank balance could stand it, I would have a brick-based greenhouse, custom built to my requirements. The brick walls would be about 76 cm (2½ ft) high, serving as a support for wooden-framed glass panels. The woodwork would be painted white and the inside walls whitewashed annually. My reason is that, notwithstanding the high initial cost, such a greenhouse is the most economical to run. Wood retains heat better than metal and brick absorbs and retains warmth very well. Also, the whitewashed inside walls would reflect the sun's rays on to the soil, to warm it quickly and thoroughly. This, after all, is the function of a greenhouse – to act as a storage cell of solar energy which costs nothing.

Of the ready-made greenhouses, my choice goes to the half-timbered, cedar wood types of traditional design, with upright sides. Here again the inside timber half-walls can be painted white for maximum heat retention and reflection. The cedar wood is weatherproofed prior to delivery and only needs treating with wood preservative once every three to five years. Also of cedar wood are the Dutchlight greenhouses. They are glass-to-ground models with outward-sloping sides to catch the sun and admit maximum light. Their main asset is that crops can be grown directly on the ground, because the glass extends

Glass to ground greenhouse with automatic watering

right down to soil level. There are also aluminium-framed greenhouses, some with upright sides and others with sides that slope slightly outwards and all are glass-to-ground structures. They are virtually maintenance free, but they do not retain warmth as well as the wooden models. However, the heat loss problem in all greenhouses can be lessened by lining the inside of the glass with polythene sheeting. The lining, of course, should not obstruct ventilation and it should be of light-gauge polythene.

Where space is limited or where a standard type greenhouse does not conform to the general garden plan, a lean-to greenhouse may be the answer. As its name suggests, it 'leans' against the side of the dwelling house. It can be of wood or aluminium and in order to trap all the sun that's going it should be erected against a south-facing wall. Because there was nowhere else to put it, I once sited a lean-to greenhouse on an east wall. I soon realized my error when the heating bills rose sharply and growth was not so good either. I took it down and sold it the following year. Properly sited, however, a 'lean-to' is not too demanding of heat. Much of the day's warmth from the sun is absorbed by the wall, retained and released slowly when the temperature drops at night. Bear in mind that you must have local authority approval before putting up a lean-to greenhouse.

A modification of the standard lean-to is a smaller version fitted with sliding doors on the long side. It is ideal for small gardens and narrow patios and costs less than the conventional lean-to greenhouse. The gardener does not actually enter the greenhouse, but tends his plants from outside through the open doors. It is excellent for growing plants, but rough on the gardener who may have to tend to them in the pouring rain.

The last type of greenhouse, in wood or metal, is the circular model. Because of its design it is a little dearer than the rectangular and lean-to models, but it does have its advantages. It permits maximum, all-round light penetration and it utilizes space to better advantage. The gardener tends his plants from the centre, being surrounded on all sides by plants on staging, or in the soil.

Siting the greenhouse

Decide where the greenhouse is to go before you buy it. It may seem stupid, but I have known someone who bought a 3.6 × 2.4-metre (12 × 8-ft) greenhouse for a site that measured approximately 3 × 2.4 metres (10 × 8 ft). What he needed was a 2.4 × 1.8-metre (8 × 6-ft) house which would allow him room to maintain the structure from the outside, i.e. he could walk round it. It is also very important to position the greenhouse in the warmest possible part of the garden. Try to avoid low-lying frost pockets, places swept by strong winds and wet, poorly drained ground. A wind-sheltered, sunny site means higher greenhouse temperatures with earlier, quicker growth all the year round.

It is also an advantage to have the greenhouse near the house where there are water and electricity already on tap. To connect both services to the greenhouse I strongly advise employing a professional to do the job, especially where electricity is involved. Do-it-yourself electrical installations are often death-traps and at best inefficient and liable to breakdowns, when heat is most needed. Lastly, try to position the greenhouse so that it runs from north to south. Sited thus, the sun passes over it from east to west and both sides of the 'house' get a fairly equal share of sunlight. But don't worry if a north-south siting is impracticable, it won't make all that much difference.

Economical greenhouse management

It is all too easy to make your greenhouse so expensive to run that your crops will cost more than those you buy. The question you have to ask yourself is whether heat is really and truly necessary? Fuel of all kinds, whether solid, gas, oil or electricity is costly and becoming dearer and in some instances less readily available. Therefore, I strongly suggest that, with vegetables in mind, heating is a luxury we can ill-afford and one that is not a necessity.

I have already shown how natural heat from the sun can be trapped, conserved and utilized in a well organized, insulated greenhouse. This solar energy is sufficient to raise excellent crops of all the vegetables we are likely to grow. They may mature a little later, but they will be no worse for that.

Solar heat, though, is not enough to germinate seeds of tender plants in spring. Even so it is not necessary to heat the whole 'house' just to germinate a few trays or pots of seeds on the staging. All you need is a good electric, thermostatically controlled propagator big enough to take from six to eight half-

trays or upwards of 40 7-cm (3-in.) peat pots at one 'sitting'. It will be big enough for all your vegetable seed-sowing requirements provided you are realistic and sow only a few more seeds than you require plants. The Dobie propagator I am currently using measures 70 cm (28 in.) in length, 63 cm (25 in.) in width and is 30 cm (12 in.) high with the transparent P.V.C. hood in position. It will take six half-trays and a few peat pots and maintains a steady pre-set temperature of up to 21°C (70°F) for less than 10p per day (at the time of writing). Those are the kind of figures I like. I have achieved the best results by covering the base with a few centimetres or so of Perlite, which is well moistened. After sowing, the trays and pots are watered and placed on the Perlite and the hood is put into position. Water evaporating from the Perlite and the compost condenses on the hood and falls back and there is no need to water the seeds until they have germinated. After germination, seedlings of the hardier vegetables are pricked-out and grown on, on the staging. The more delicate seedlings such as cucumbers, melons and sweet peppers are pricked-out singly into 7-cm (3-in.) pots and grown on, in the propagator, for a few weeks. When plants are being grown in the propagator, the rubber plugs are removed from the ventilation holes in the hood, to improve air circulation and freshness. I reckon the initial cost of the propagator is recouped in, at most, two years in terms of staging into a giant propagator as I have described on p. 45.
staging into a giant propagator as I have described on p. oo.

I realize that some gardeners may wish to heat their greenhouses to achieve earlier crops. For them I suggest paraffin as the most convenient and as one of the most economical fuels. A blue-flame paraffin heater, provided it is big enough for the job, will prove an effective frost barrier on the coldest nights. It will also suffice to raise the 'house' temperature several degrees above those pertaining outside. The custom-made paraffin greenhouse heaters are equipped with water trays. These should be kept filled to prevent the atmosphere becoming too dry.

Electrical heating equipment may be either tubular, or of the forced draught type. Of the two, the forced draught fan-heaters are very expensive to run even though, like the tubular heaters, they are thermostatically controlled. Mains-gas and bottled-gas heaters are also available and, in general, they are the cheapest form of heating, being more economical even than paraffin. It is worth bearing in mind, however, that the cost of the gas and electrical equipment and its installation can be high. In conclusion, I strongly advocate low-cost vegetable production achieved in an insulated brick or panel-based cold greenhouse, using a propagator for seed germination.

Good greenhouse management

New greenhouse owners often labour under the misapprehension that the higher the temperature, the earlier and the better the crops will be. They keep their greenhouses closed, or only poorly ventilated, even on hot, sunny days. In fact, very high temperatures and inadequate ventilation are not in the plants' interests. Surprising as it may seem, an air temperature of over 26°C (80°F) tends to inhibit the ripening of tomatoes rather than encourage it.

Ventilation

Fungus diseases pose a threat to all greenhouse-grown vegetables. They are most likely to attack plants that are growing in a hot, humid and still atmosphere. Following the principle that prevention is better than cure, our aim is to keep the air inside the greenhouse moving and buoyant. Ideally, the 'house' should have at least one roof ventilator and, if possible, another on one side, near ground level. On very cold, cloudy days all ventilators may be closed down to conserve warmth. But even in the depths of winter, the inside temperature may rise to over 15°C (60°F) when the sun is shining and the rise can occur in a matter of minutes. If you are at home when the weather conditions change, there is no problem; you merely open the ventilators and close them again when the outside temperature drops. However, proper ventilation can be a problem when there is no one around to make the necessary adjustments. Automatic ventilator-openers are the simple answer. They are easily fitted, to either top or side ventilators, and require no power, other than the sun's warmth, to operate them. They are, basically, expansion rods that expand and contract according to the air temperature. They can be adjusted to allow the ventilators to start opening at whatever temperature you wish, and, properly fitted, they are trouble-free and cost nothing to run. The greenhouse door is also a ventilator and can be left open if the temperature soars to 21°C (70°F) and over.

Watering

All plants need water. Without it they are unable to feed, as they take their plant foods from the soil in solution. Water flowing through their veins also keeps plants turgid and at maximum growth. When there is insufficient water plants suffer from wilting which affects them in two stages. The first stage is 'incipient wilt' and if water is given fairly quickly, the plants will recover and be very little worse for the temporary set-back. Repeated incipient wilt will eventually result in a severe growth check. The second stage is 'permanent wilt', the point of no return, when no amount of water will save the plant from dying.

Although plants must have water to survive, they can die just as surely from overwatering as they can from thirst. Overwatering the soil drives the air out and it becomes a sodden, stagnant medium in which the roots suffocate. The ideal is an evenly moist soil where the roots can find plenty of water to keep pace with the volume of water loss through the leaves. Small, young plants need less water than large ones so adjust your watering to meet their varying requirements. Unless you can be sure you are available to give water when it is needed, you may consider installing an automatic system. The simplest system, adequate for pot plants, is to stand them on an absorbant surface on the staging. Water reaches the roots by capillary action. The absorbent material can be an inch or two of peat, that should be changed every year or so, or a special capillary matting. The second system is trickle irrigation, involving a drip-feed water supply to each individual plant. A liquid fertilizer may be added to the trickle irrigation system, if required.

Growing pains

Insect pests and fungus diseases can play havoc in the greenhouse. Keep a close watch on your plants and, if trouble strikes, deal with it at once. The longer you leave it, the worse it gets. Liquid sprays and pesticidal dusts are readily available to deal with all the problems you are likely to encounter. Most of these are described in a later chapter (*see* pp. 145 to 156).

Dealing with pests

The most effective way of dealing with greenhouse pests is by fumigation as the fine 'smoke' penetrates to every nook and cranny. To fumigate, work out the cubic area of your greenhouse, then buy the appropriate number of smoke 'bombs'. Choose a still, dull day, place the 'bombs' at regular intervals along the path and light the blue paper, starting with the bomb furthest from the door, so that you can retreat and leave the 'house', without breathing the smoke. Also, see that all the ventilators are shut and stop up any gaps in the glass or under the door with sacking or newspaper. Leave for a few hours for the fumigant to do its work, then open up and return everything to normal. It is usually advisable to fumigate a second time, one week later.

If you are not quite sure how you work out the cubic capacity of your greenhouse, this is the calculation that you have to work out: the length, multiplied by the width, multiplied by the height from ground level to the half-way point between eaves and ridge.

In the autumn, when the greenhouse is virtually at rest, it pays to wash the woodwork and glass with disinfectant. But, a word of warning, never use creosote to preserve the woodwork. The fumes emitted from creosote will kill most plants. Instead, use Cuprinol wood preservative or ordinary, household paint.

Methods of shading

Too much direct sunlight and too high temperatures can also prove harmful to plants and some form of shading is desirable. I have always found that weak lime wash does a good job, as it reduces the power of the sun's rays without cutting out too much natural light. I put a couple of handfuls of lime into a bucket of water and stir it to an even consistency. Using a distemper brush, I paint one pane of glass on the outside and leave it to dry. If the resulting shading looks about right, I carry on painting the rest of the glass panes; if it doesn't I dilute, or strengthen, the 'solution' as the case may be until I am satisfied with the result. There are also some proprietary shading substances available that, used at the recommended dilutions, leave a thin coating of green shading. The only snag with these materials, either limewash or the special preparations, is their comparative permanence. During long spells of dull weather they may obstruct more light than is desirable. Ideally, the shading should be adjustable to suit weather conditions, a simple matter if you fit roller blinds manufactured specially for the purpose. On dull days they remain unfurled, whereas when the sun is beating down from a clear, blue sky they can be pulled down to give just the right amount of shade.

Watering and ventilation

The last word on good greenhouse management concerns maintaining the correct balance between watering and ventilation. More fungus diseases occur due to incorrect watering than to any other causes. During the daytime greenhouse plants grow best in a warm and fairly humid atmosphere that is also buoyant. Very warm, dry air increases their rate of transpiration (water loss through the leaves) to a point beyond which growth is retarded. During the night plants need and use less water and their rate of growth is slower. Also, the ventilation is reduced to conserve warmth. Bearing these factors in mind, watering should be done in the morning. Plants in pots and in the beds need to be given enough water to satisfy their needs for the day. In addition, the area under the staging and the paths should be well soaked with water to avoid an arid atmosphere. With the ventilators open and the air warm, moist and in circulation the plants will be supremely happy. The worst thing you can do is to water late in the afternoon, or evening, shortly before closing the greenhouse down for the night. The humid air thus created will fail to escape and as the outside temperature drops, the moisture will condense on the inside of the glass. In such a dank atmosphere, with the inside temperature also dropping, fungus diseases gain a foothold.

Good plant growth results from good greenhouse management, itself based on warmth, in a fresh-air environment, with the plants' different day and night requirements taken into consideration.

SEED-SOWING CHART

	When to sow				When to plant outdoors	Distances apart	
Vegetable	Outdoors in rows	Outdoors under cloches	Outdoors in seed beds	In heated greenhouse		In rows	Between rows
Asparagus			April		Sept-Oct	60 cm (2ft)	60 cm (2ft)
Aubergine				Feb-March	June	In single 20-cm (9-in) pots	
Bean, broad	Feb-March and Oct	February				20 cm (9 in)	60-90 cm (2-3 ft)
Bean, dwarf, french	late April and May	March-April		March	late May-June	20 cm (9 in)	60 cm (2 ft)
Bean, runner	May	April		April	late May-June	30 cm (1 ft)	90 cm (3 ft)
Beetroot	April-July	March-April				15 cm (6 in)	20 cm (9 in)
Beet, spinach	April-May	March				20 cm (9 in)	38 cm (15 in)
Beet, sea kale	April-June	March				20 cm (9 in)	45 cm (18 in)

Beet, rhubarb chard	April-June	March				20 cm (9 in)	45 cm (18 in)
Borecole (kale)			April-May		July-Aug	60 cm (2 ft)	60 cm (2 ft)
Broccoli, sprouting			late March and April		June-July	45 cm (18 in)	45 cm (18 in)
Brussels sprouts			March-April		May-July	60 cm (2 ft)	60 cm (2 ft)
Cabbage, summer		March	March-April		April-July	45 cm (18 in)	60 cm (2 ft)
Cabbage, winter			April-June		May-July	45 cm (18 in)	45 cm (18 in)
Cabbage, spring			mid-July to mid-Aug		Sept and early Oct	45 cm (18 in)	45cm (18in)
Cardoon		April-May			June-July	45 cm (18 in)	120cm (4ft)
Capsicum (peppers)				March-April	late May and June	45 cm (18 in)	45 cm (18 in)
Carrot	March-July	Feb-March				5-7 cm (2-3 in)	20 cm (9 in)

	When to sow				When to plant outdoors	Distances apart	
Vegetable	**Outdoors in rows**	**Outdoors under cloches**	**Outdoors in seed beds**	**In heated greenhouse**		**In rows**	**Between rows**
Cauliflower		Feb-March	March-May	February	April-June	45 cm (18 in)	45 cm (18 in)
Celery, self-blanching				March	late May and June	20 cm (9in)	30 cm (1 ft)
Celery, blanching				March	late May and June	20 cm (9 in)	120 cm (4 ft)
Celeriac				March	late May and June	20 cm (9 in)	30 cm (1 ft)
Chicory	June					20 cm (9 in)	30 cm (1 ft)
Cress	In warmth all the year round						
Cucumber, outdoor				March-April	June	45 cm (18 in)	45 cm (18 in)
Cucumber, indoor				March		one plant is enough for the average greenhouse	
Endive	June-July					30 cm (1 ft)	30 cm (1 ft)

Garlic					from bulbs in March	20 cm (9 in)	20 cm (9 in)
Kohl rabi	April-May					15 cm (6 in)	20 cm (9 in)
Leek		March	March-April	Feb-March	May-July	20 cm (9 in)	30 cm (1 ft)
Lettuce, summer	March-July	March		Feb-March	March-April	15-30 cm (6-12 in)	30 cm (1 ft)
Lettuce, winter	Aug-Oct					20-30 cm (9-12 in)	20 cm (9 in)
Marrow		May		April	June	120 cm (4 ft)	120-150 cm (4-5 ft)
Melon •				April	June in frames or cloches	90-120 cm (3-4 ft)	90-120 cm (3-4 ft)
Mustard	In warmth all the year round						
Onion, from sets	Feb-April				Feb-May	15 cm (6in)	20 cm (9 in)
Onion, from seeds	March-April	Feb-March		Jan-March	April	15-20 cm (6-9 in)	20 cm (9 in)
Onion, pickling	March	February				unthinned	20 cm (9 in)

	When to sow				When to plant outdoors	Distances apart	
Vegetable	**Outdoors in rows**	**Outdoors under cloches**	**Outdoors in seed beds**	**In heated greenhouse**		**In rows**	**Between rows**
Onion, Welsh			March		April	20 cm (9 in)	30 cm (1 ft)
Parsley	March-Aug	March				10-15 cm (4-6 in)	20 cm (9 in)
Parsnip	March-April					15 cm (6in)	30 cm (1 ft)
Pea	March-July	Feb-March Oct-Nov				5-7 cm (2-3 in)	45-60 cm (1½-2 ft)
Potato					March-May	20-38 cm (9-15 in)	45-60 cm (1½-2 ft)
Pumpkin		May		March-April	late May-June	one or two plants spaced 180 cm (6ft) apart	
Radish	March-June	Feb-March				7 cm (3 in)	15 cm (6in)
Rhubarb		March	March-April	Feb-March	Sept-Oct	90 cm (3 ft)	90 cm (3 ft)
Salsify	April-May					20 cm (9 in)	20-30 cm (9-12 in)

Scorzonera	April-May					20 cm (9 in)	20-30 cm (9-12 in)
Shallot					Jan-May	15 cm (6 in)	15 cm (6in)
Spinach, summer	March-June	March				15 cm (6 in)	30 cm (1 ft)
Spinach, winter	July-Sept					15 cm (6 in)	30 cm (1 ft)
Spinach, New Zealand		April		March-April	late May-June	90 cm (3 ft)	90 cm (3 ft)
Swede	April-May					30 cm (1 ft)	45 cm (1½ ft)
Turnip	March-July	Feb-March				15 cm (6 in)	30 cm (1 ft)
Sweet corn		May		March-April	late May-June	60 cm (2 ft)	60 cm (2 ft)
Tomato				Jan-April	late May-June	60 cm (2 ft)	60 cm (2 ft)

6

VEGETABLES, A to Z

Preface

In this chapter I have tried to present each vegetable as the individual it is. Each has its own likes and dislikes, its own pests and problems and its own characteristic responses to any given treatment. Following the name of the vegetable, I have appended its group designation, as it is related to its nutritional needs and to its place in the crop rotation system, where this applies.

Under each heading are listed the pests and diseases that can affect that particular vegetable, but the measures to combat them are considered in more detail in Chapter 7 (*see* p. 145). I have also included a little information on exhibiting vegetables, for the many readers who will want to show-off the excellence of the produce they have grown.

When assessing the merits of vegetables, judges are aided by the guidelines laid down by The Royal Horticultural Society in *The Horticultural Show Handbook**. Points are awarded for condition, size, uniformity and colour, up to a variable maximum, related to the level of expertise required to grow each vegetable to a high standard. I have indicated the maximum points each vegetable can merit in this scale, to assist exhibitors who intend staging vegetable collections. For the housewife, I have also included the blanching time each vegetable requires prior to deep-freezing.

Artichoke

There are two distinct kinds of artichoke, the globe artichoke and the Jerusalem artichoke. They differ widely, both in use and in appearance.

*Published by the Royal Horticultural Society, Vincent Square, London SW1P 2PE.

Globe artichoke

Although the globe artichoke will not be found in the small-town greengrocer's shop, it is easy to grow, if you have the room for it. Being a large, tall plant it needs a spacing of 1.2 metres (4 ft) between the rows and the plants in the rows. It also likes a deep, rich soil and a warm place in which to grow, sheltered from winds. It may be obtained and propagated in two ways. In spring you can buy rooted plants that should be planted immediately and the flower buds nipped off when small, in the first year, to allow the plants to become established. In the second year the edible flower heads may be cut for cooking just before the flowers open. To replace old plants and to increase your existing stock is easy. Each plant develops a number of suckers around the base. Three or four of these suckers, about 20 cm (9 in.) long, may be taken from each plant, in April. Choose the strongest suckers and make sure each has a small piece of root attached to it, then plant in the normal way.

Globe artichokes may also be grown from seeds sown in warmth in February, or in a seed bed outdoors, in March and April. Plants grown from seed vary from good to poor so, for permanent planting in autumn, select the strongest youngsters and discard the weak, spindly ones.

Good varieties: Green Ball, Green Globe
Pests and/or diseases: usually trouble-free
Blanching time: 8 to 10 minutes

Exhibition points:	Condition	4
(thick, fleshy scales and large,	Size	4
well-shaped and heavy heads)	Solidity	4
	Uniformity	3
		15

Jerusalem artichoke

Jerusalem artichokes grow to 2.7 to 3 metres (9 to 10 ft) tall and are often used as a hedge to screen off a compost heap or bin. They are bought as tubers vaguely resembling knobbly potatoes. The tubers may be planted 15 cm (6 in.) deep and 30 cm (12 in.) apart in rows 60 cm (2 ft) apart, either in October or in

February and March. They do not need earthing-up and they are ready for lifting when the leaves turn yellow and begin to die back. The largest and best tubers are stored in sand or peat for eating during the winter as required. Small tubers are also stored for replanting in spring.

Good variety: Fuseau
Pests and/or diseases: usually trouble-free
Exhibition points:
(large, well-shaped tubers with smooth, clean skins)

Condition	2
Size	2
Shape	4
Uniformity	2
	10

Asparagus
Asparagus will not tolerate a wet, soggy soil and only gives good crops on a rich, well-drained site. As the plants are perennial and will occupy the same piece of ground for many years, it pays to dig in plenty of well-rotted manure or compost when preparing the bed.

Asparagus may either be grown from seed or from 'crowns' bought from a reliable supplier. For people in a hurry I recommend buying two-year-old crowns that will yield usable 'spears' in the second year after planting. Plants raised from seed take three years before cutting can begin. Crowns are planted 15 cm (6 in.) deep in March or April, spacing them 45 cm (1½ ft) apart all round. While the plants are becoming established the space between them can be used to grow such things as lettuce, or spring onions, as catch crops. When the feathery leaves turn yellow in the autumn, cut the stems right back almost to ground level and top dress the bed with a 10 cm (4 in.) layer of well-rotted 'organics'. In March, when growth is just beginning, dust the bed over with 'Blood, Fish and Bone' fertilizer at 56 grams (2 oz) to the square metre.

Asparagus shoots from mature plants are ready for cutting when there is about 10 cm (4 in.) of growth above the soil. Take a long, sharp knife and cut the shoots just above the crown, about 5 to 7 cm (2 to 3 in.) below the soil. Cut only the nice, thick shoots or 'spears' and leave the thin ones to nourish the plants. All cutting should cease after the first, or second, week in June to give the crowns a chance to build up their reserves ready for the following year.

To grow from seed, sow in March or April in a seed bed, after first soaking the seed for 24 hours in water, to soften the hard seed coat. When the seedlings have made four leaves, thin them to 7 cm (3 in.) apart and finally plant them into the prepared bed in the autumn.

Good varieties: Connover's Colossal, Early Argenteuil
Pests and/or diseases: asparagus beetle
Blanching time: 2 to 4 minutes

Exhibition points:	Condition	6
(long, thick straight spears with	Size	6
tightly closed scales)	Uniformity	3
		15

Aubergine (egg plant)
Aubergines belong to the same plant family as the tomato and require very similar growing conditions. They may either be grown from seed-sowing to maturity in a greenhouse, or in pots or growing-bags outdoors from early June onwards, in the warmest, sunniest part of the garden.

Sow the seeds in warmth from January to March singly in 7-cm (3-in) pots in a minimum temperature of 15°C (60°F). If you intend to grow your aubergines in the greenhouse bed, plant them when they are about 10 cm (4 in.) tall. For pot cultivation, pot the seedlings on, first into 12- or 15-cm (5- or 6-in.) pots and finally into 26-cm (10-in.) pots, using a good potting compost. Aubergines will also grow well in growing bags with a south-facing wall or fence behind them.

To obtain a good crop, pinch out the main growing tip, when the plant is 30 to 38 cm (12 to 15 in.) high. It will then branch out and should be restricted to only two lateral branches. They, in turn, should be stopped when they are 15 cm (6 in.) long. Each plant is capable of carrying up to six fruits and once this number of flowers has set and the fruits are forming all other laterals should be nipped in the bud.

Good varieties: Early Long Purple, Slim Jim
Pests and/or diseases: usually trouble-free
Blanching time: 4 minutes

Exhibition points:	Condition	8
(large, clean, deeply-coloured	Size	3
and firm fruits)	Uniformity	4
		15

Bean, broad (legume group)

Broad beans are a wasteful crop, as 75 per cent of what you pick you throw away, leaving only the beans for cooking. However, if they are gathered young when the pods are only about 10 cm (4 in.) long and the bean seeds inside are beginning to form, they can be cooked and eaten whole and are delicious. The taller varieties grow to 120 to 150 cm (4 to 5 ft) high. For small gardens the dwarf varieties are less space demanding, growing as they do to a mere 38 cm (15 in.) in height. There are also one or two varieties that may be sown in October or November to overwinter and crop in the early summer sooner than varieties sown at the more usual time in spring. They are, however, at risk from prolonged, hard frosts and need cloche protection to ensure their survival.

Spring sowing can start in February under cloches and may continue at intervals right through to May. By successional sowing you can enjoy continuous feeds of broad beans right through the summer. To sow, take out a shallow trench about 2 cm (1 in.) deep and the width of the spade. Into the trench, sow the seeds 20 cm (9 in.) apart, along each side, alternating them from side to side. Cover them over with soil and firm it down with the back of the spade. Allow 60 cm (2 ft) between rows of tall varieties and 45 cm (1½ ft) between rows of the dwarf ones. Although broad beans are strong plants they can be blown over in high winds, especially if they are wet with rain. To prevent this happening, place canes at 2.4 to 3 metre (8 to 10 ft) intervals down each side of the row and run a few lengths of strong twine between them. The pods should be picked when they are fresh and green and before they age and show signs of reddish-brown staining. The most common pest of broad beans is black fly. This pest concentrates its attacks on the growing tips only. As soon as you see signs of it, pinch off 5 or 7 cm (2 or 3 in.) of the growing point and your troubles will be over. It is worth noting that plants from autumn and very early spring sowings often escape attack because they have finished cropping before the black fly arrives.

Good varieties: for autumn sowing, Aquadulce; for spring sowing, Rentpayer, Promotion, Imperial, Green Windsor, Bonny Lad (dwarf)
Pests and/or diseases: black fly, bean weevil, pea and bean moth
Blanching time: 3 minutes

Exhibition points:	Condition	6
(large, green, many-seeded pods	Size	5
that are at peak maturity)	Uniformity	4
		15

Beans, dwarf French (legume group)

To many people dwarf French beans are but the poor relations of runner beans. It is true they have a more subdued flavour, but, as they may be sown and harvested earlier than 'runners', it is worth putting a row in.

Seeds may be sown under cloches in early April or in the open ground from the end of the month until the end of June. Sow them in a 2-cm (1-in.) deep, 30-cm (12-in.) wide trench, spacing the seeds 10 to 15 cm (4 to 6 in.) apart. Although they are short stemmed and rarely exceed 60 cm (2 ft) in height, dwarf French beans need a little support, especially if they are cropping heavily, otherwise the plants tend to flop over after wind and rain. All they need is a length of strong twine, attached to short sticks, run down each side of the row. As soon as they begin to flower start looking for ripe, tender pods about 15 cm (6 in.) long. They tend to be hidden under the ample leaves and are easily missed. Pick the pods young and the plants will continue to crop for several weeks.

Earlier crops of dwarf French beans may be enjoyed from sowings made in the greenhouse in February and March. Sow four seeds in a 25-cm (10-in.) pot of rich soil and keep them watered and fed with a liquid fertilizer as they grow.

Good varieties: Tendergreen, Cordon, Earligreen
Pests and/or diseases: aphids
Blanching time: whole beans, 2 to 3 minutes; sliced beans, 1 minute

Exhibition points: (the pods should be straight, even, clean and should snap cleanly under gentle finger pressure)		
	Condition	6
	Size	3
	Form	3
	Uniformity	3
		15

Bean, haricot (legume group)
Haricot beans are grown in exactly the same way as dwarf French beans. Where they differ is that the pods are left on the plants until they are brown and dried. When they reach this stage the plants are lifted and hung in a dry, airy shed or garage. When the pods are light yellow in colour and parchment dry, they are shelled and the beans are spread out on sheets of paper to finish drying off. When they are perfectly dry, put them into lidded containers or paper bags. Before using, soak the beans in water overnight to soften them prior to cooking.

Good varieties: Chevrier Vert, Purley King
Pests and/or diseases: aphids

Bean, runner (legume group)
If I had room in the garden for only one vegetable, the one I would grow would be runner beans. A well-grown row will yield a prolific crop of beans, that are delicious eaten fresh or used from the freezer. It is a vegetable that needs a deep, rich soil and one for which it is worth digging deep trenches. One of the problems with runner beans is that in some years the flowers drop off before they 'set'. Many and varied reasons have been put forward for this weakness, which I believe stems from the sub-tropical origins of the plant. In their natural home runner beans are accustomed to permanently moist soils and a humid atmosphere. Our aim, therefore, should be to reproduce these conditions as nearly as possible in our gardens. My runner beans never fail to set, due, I am sure, to the treatment they receive.

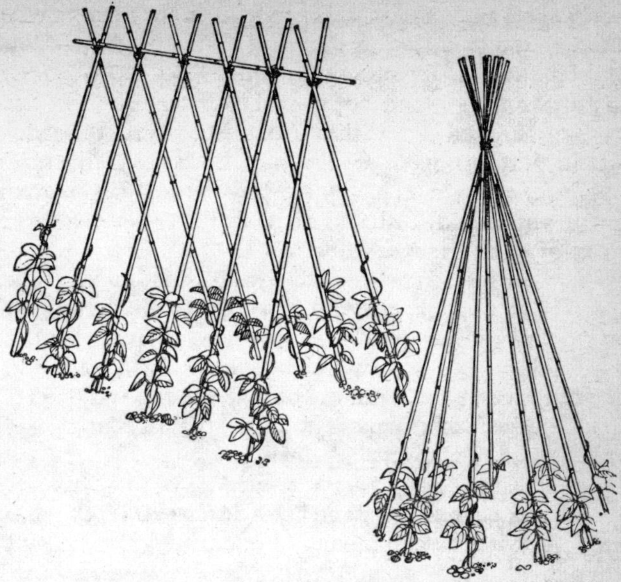

Support system for runner beans

Preparations begin in November or December. I take out a trench 45 to 60 cm (1½ to 2 ft) deep and 45 cm (1½ ft) wide. Into the bottom I put, first, a 10- to 15-cm (4- to 6-in.) layer of old newspaper soaked in water and then a 30-cm (1-ft) deep layer of manure or compost, finishing off with a dusting of bone meal at 28 g (1 oz) to the metre run of row. The soil is replaced up to its original level, but it is not firmed down, but left to settle in its own time. When the end of April comes along I am ready to put the supporting canes in. At this stage the level of the soil in the trench has sunk several inches below the surrounding ground. If it needs it, I top up with soil until the trench level is about 7 cm (3 in.) below soil level, leaving a shallow depression along its length. Then 2.4 metre (8 ft) long canes are pushed in, opposite each other, along both sides of the trench, at 30 cm (1 ft) spacings. Then, beginning at one end, the tops of the canes are overlapped to form a V, into which is inserted a horizontal cane to keep the upright canes crossed about 30 cm below their tips. The upright and horizontal canes are then securely tied where they meet.

In the meantime, runner bean seeds were sown under closed cloches, in the seed bed, in the third week of April, to produce plants for putting out on, or near, June 1. A week before planting, the trench receives its last soil treatment, 26 to 56 grams (1 to 2 oz) of 'Blood, Fish and Bone' fertilizer per metre run, hoed into the top few centimetres. In due course I put one plant in at the foot of each cane and keep a handful in reserve, lest any fail to 'take'. From this point on, the only attention the runner beans get is water, which they need in large quantities in dry weather. But I never spray the leaves with cold water. When the need arises, I put the hose at one end and flood the trench. The wet soil emanates humidity that rises up through the plants and the flowers 'set' freely.

Seeds may also be sown *in situ* in late May or early June, one seed at the foot of each cane and half a dozen extra at the end of the row as possible gap fillers. Alternatively, seeds may be sown, one per 3-in. pot, in April or May in the greenhouse.

Good varieties: Prizewinner Enorma, Achievement, Fry, Streamline
Pests and/or diseases: black fly, slugs
Blanching time: 2 minutes (sliced)

Exhibition points:		
(pods should be long, straight, clean	Condition	8
and showing no outward sign of seed	Size	3
formation; they should snap easily	Form	3
and cleanly)	Uniformity	4
		18

Beetroot (rootcrop group)

Growing beetroot is easy; growing good beetroot is a little more difficult. Over the years I have learnt that it is a mistake to sow too early, unless you can give cloche protection. Early sowings tend to germinate badly, due to low soil temperatures and many of those that do germinate run to seed.

The first requirement for good beetroot is a soil that is rich in organic material and in plant foods. At all stages of growth, from tiny seedling to edible root, the beetroot needs plenty of food and soil moisture. If either are in short supply for any length of time, the plants 'bolt', i.e. run to seed, prematurely. So dig in ample 'organics' during winter and early spring, top dress with a general 'concentrate' prior to sowing and drench the rows with water in dry spells.

Start sowing under cloches in early April and keep the cloches over the plants until the leaves touch the top. In the open ground, sow successionally from late April through to July and pull the beetroots when they are young and about the size of a golf ball, if it is a round variety. There are also varieties with long, tapering roots and intermediate varieties that have nicely shaped, cylindrical roots. Note, also, that the beetroot 'seed' you normally buy is, in fact, a seed cluster containing many seeds. Therefore, sow the clusters thinly, spacing them about 3 in. apart, because you will probably get more than one seedling from each cluster. On the other hand, pelleted beetroot contain only one seed per pellet, the cluster having been dismembered prior to the pelleting process.

As they are tender plants any beetroot still in the ground in September should be lifted before the frost gets them. Pull them up, twist the leaves off, clean them of soil and store them for winter use in boxes of peat or sand, placed in a frost and vermin-free place.

Good varieties:

Round roots, Boltardy, Detroit Little Ball, Burpees' Golden (orange colour)

Long roots, Cheltenham Greentop

Cylindrical roots, Housewives' Choice

Pests and/or diseases: usually trouble-free

Blanching time: small roots, 15 minutes (boil); large, mature roots, 45 minutes (boil)

Exhibition points:
(globe varieties should be evenly round with small tap roots. The flesh should be a good, deep colour with little or no 'rings' and firm. Skins unblemished)

Condition	5
Colour of flesh	6
Uniformity	4
	15

Beet, seakale or Swiss chard

Seakale beet is grown for its succulent, edible stems and leaves. The stems are thick and white and are cooked in the same way as asparagus and the leaves are cooked like spinach. Sow the seeds outdoors from April to mid-May, in rows 45 cm (1½ ft) apart. Thin the seedlings to 20 cm (9 in.) apart when they have grown four leaves. When harvesting, do not cut the stems and leaves, pull them; in this way more stems and leaves will form and you can continue cropping well into autumn.

Good variety: Swiss Chard
Pests and/or diseases: usually trouble-free

Beet, rhubarb chard

The main difference between rhubarb chard and seakale beet is the leaf colour, which in rhubarb chard is a deep and brilliant red. In every other respect treat it as you would seakale beet.

Good variety: Rhubarb Chard
Pests and/or diseases: usually trouble-free

Beet, perpetual spinach

This is another beet that is grown for its edible leaves. Many gardeners prefer it to summer spinach because it will withstand long, dry spells without running to seed. It is also an almost all-the-year-round vegetable. Seeds sown in April and May will provide a summer crop, and further sowings made in July will yield fresh leaves for cooking in winter. As the plants are large and leafy allow 38 cm (15 in.) between rows and 20 cm (9 in.) between plants in the rows.

Good variety: Perpetual Spinach
Pests and/or diseases: usually trouble-free

Borecole or kale (brassica group)

Because of its extreme hardiness borecole is popular in Scotland and in other areas that experience severe winters. The leaves are tough, thick and curled and have a strong cabbage flavour when cooked. It is an extremely useful fresh vegetable for use in the dead of winter when greens are scarce and expensive.

Sow the seeds in the seed bed in April or early May and plant the young plants out in July and August in rows 60 cm (2 ft) apart with 60 cm also between the plants in the rows.

Good varieties: Frosty, Dwarf Green Curled
Pests and/or diseases: caterpillars, root fly, club root

Broccoli (brassica group)
The purple and white sprouting broccoli are good 'hungry gap' vegetables coming to maturity in the lean months of March and April when the winter 'greens' are finished and the spring cabbages are not ready. Seeds are sown in the seed bed in April and the young plants put out in July, in rows, allowing 60 cm (2 ft) apart all round. To make good use of space, I usually plant mine in ground that becomes available after early potatoes or peas have been harvested. Although fairly weather resistant, sprouting broccoli can be decimated and killed by a combination of hard frost and high winds. Therefore, they need to be strong plants by the time winter sets in. For this reason, plant them in good soil, but give them no additional fertilizer and, in particular, no nitrogenous fertilizer that would only make for soft growth.

In exposed gardens it is worth protecting the plants with sheets of polythene down each side of the row. The long, tender flower stalks that appear in the spring should be cut when they snap easily and long before the flowers open. They should also be cooked immediately after cutting to get the best of their lovely flavour.

There is also a summer-ready broccoli called calabrese, which I believe is very under-rated. Seeds sown in the seed bed in April will yield plants that crop by about September or a little earlier. They first of all produce a central head of tight green-coloured florets about 10 to 15 cm (4 to 6 in.) across. After cutting the head you then get a succession of mouth-watering green sprouts for a period of about six weeks.

Another broccoli that used to be more popular than it is now is the perennial variety. Each plant grows a central head in spring and this is followed by a succession of from six to nine smaller but equally tasty heads. All the heads should be cut and used before they flower to prevent the plants from seeding and dying. When well grown and regularly cropped the plants can be expected to live and yield worthwhile crops for about five years. Seeds are sown in the seed bed in April or May and the plants put out later on, allowing 90 cm (3 ft) between them.

Good varieties: Early Purple Sprouting, White Sprouting, Corvet (an F_1 hybrid), Green Sprouting and Nine Star Perennial
Pests and/or diseases: caterpillars, root fly, club root, white fly
Blanching time: 3 to 4 minutes
Exhibition points: all types merit a maximum of 15 points (heads and/or sprouts should be closely clustered and fresh, and leaves should be green, crisp and clean)

Brussels sprouts (brassica group)
In a well-planned garden there are Brussels sprouts for the picking from September right through to the following March. There are early, mid-season and late varieties and the early ones can be sown in succession and come into yield in sequence.

Seeds are sown in early March under cloches and from late March to late April in the open seed bed. Sow thinly and plant out when the plants have four good leaves and they are about 15 cm (6 in.) tall. Dwarf varieties should be spaced at 45 cm (1½ ft) and the taller ones at 60 cm (2 ft) apart each way (in the rows and between the rows). After planting, firm the soil hard around the roots and, in the case of tall varieties, tie each plant to a stout cane to prevent it rocking loose, or even toppling over in strong winds.

Harvest the sprouts from the bottom of the stalk upwards when they are nice and tightly 'buttoned'. Sprouts always taste sweeter when they have had a frost or two to bring out their fine flavour. When all the sprouts have been picked, don't throw the plants away before eating the top leaves – they are delicious.

Good varieties:
Early – Peer Gynt (an F_1 hybrid), Early Dwarf
Mid-season – Roodnerf Perfection, Prince Askold (an F_1 hybrid)
Late – New Year, Fasolt (an F_1 hybrid)
Pests and/or diseases: caterpillars, root fly, club root, white fly
Blanching time: 3 minutes
Exhibition points:
(sprouts should be tight, fresh and solid and not discoloured)

Condition	6
Solidity	5
Uniformity	4
	15

Cabbage (brassica group)
Cabbage is the great British standby, cooked, all too often in too much water, for too long, until it becomes an evil-smelling, yellow-green mush. Steamed in a little water for about 15 minutes, it retains its colour, firmness and excellent flavour. By growing selected varieties it is possible to cut a fresh cabbage from the garden almost every week of the year. They all like a firm and fertile soil with lime in it, and their seeds need to be sown in the seed bed at the right time to suit the variety. They need copious watering in dry weather and are better if they are earthed-up as they grow. Earthing helps to keep them secure in the soil and they will also send out new roots into the soil.

Summer cabbage
Seeds are sown in a seed bed from March to June, and the young plants are put out about 45 to 60 cm (1½ to 2 ft) apart in rows. Some varieties have pointed heads, others are round and all should be cut as soon as they are hard and firm. As far as I know the quickest-maturing cabbage is the F_1 hybrid Hispi, which is ready to cut in ten weeks from sowing. Hispi may also be sown under cloches and in frames in September and October. The seedlings are left unthinned and are planted out in March to yield a very early crop. If you leave the stalk in the ground after cutting the cabbage, you will get baby cabbages from it. All you do is cut a ½-inch deep cross in the top end of the stalk and you will soon be cutting three or four small, loose-leaf and delicious secondary heads.

Winter cabbage

Seeds are sown in a seed bed from April to early June and the plants put out 45 cm (1½ ft) apart each way in June and July. Winter cabbages can be usefully planted in ground vacated by earlier crops after first giving the ground a scattering of general fertilizer. Plant firmly and earth up as they grow.

Spring cabbage

Seeds are sown in a seed bed in late July in the North and in early August in the South. In dry weather it will be necessary to water the seed bed every evening, to ensure good germination. When they are about 15 cm (6 in.) tall (in September or October) the plants are put out 30 cm (12 in.) apart in rows 45 cm (1½ ft) apart. The closer planting gives them a measure of mutual weather protection. Plant them in fertile soil manured for a previous crop, but give them no additional fertilizer. To survive the winter the plants must be hardy and should not be soft-leaved. The time to give them a fertilizer boost is in the spring when growth restarts. Then give them a teaspoonful each of sulphate of ammonia to get them moving.

Red cabbage

Red cabbage is grown in the same way as ordinary summer cabbage. Its virtue is that it is excellent for pickling in vinegar after an overnight salting. Pickled red cabbage is delicious with cold meats, cheese and in winter salads.

Good varieties:

Summer cabbage – Hispi (an F_1 hybrid, pointed head), Market Topper (an F_1 hybrid, ballhead), Golden Acre (ballhead), Winningstadt (pointed head)

Winter cabbage – Celtic (an F_1 hybrid, ballhead), Savoy-Ice Queen (an F_1 hybrid, ballhead), January King (ballhead), Christmas Drumhead (ballhead)

Spring cabbage – April, Offenham–Flower of Spring

Red cabbage – Niggy, Red Drumhead

Pests and/or diseases: caterpillars, root fly, club root, white fly

Blanching time: 2 to 4 minutes

Exhibition points: (hearts should be firm, tight and fresh and of good shape. Outer leaves should be clean and not too large)	Condition	6
	Firmness	5
	Uniformity	4
		15

Capsicum or sweet pepper

Both red and green peppers are one and the same variety, picked from the same plants. It is just that the green fruits turn red if they are left on the plants to ripen.

Seeds are sown in March, in a temperature of 15°C to 18°C (60°F to 65°F), sowing two seeds in each 7-cm (3-in.) compost-filled pot. If both seeds germinate remove the weakest and leave the other to grow on. When the plants have grown six leaves you have to decide how and where you wish to grow them. If you settle for pot culture, transplant the seedling into a 20- or 22-cm (8- or 9-in.) pot of John Innes No. 2 potting compost. The pot may be left in the greenhouse throughout the summer, or it may be put outside from the middle of June, in the warmest, sunniest part of the garden. A good place is at the foot of a south-facing wall.

I prefer to grow mine, three plants to a growing bag with a warm wall behind them. After planting and putting them out in early June, the bag is covered with a Stewart cloche and this is left in position until the plants touch the top. The reason for the added protection is that peppers are not quite as hardy as tomatoes, although they both belong to the same plant family (the *Solanaceae*). They appreciate the extra warmth of the cloche and, as a result, they crop earlier and better. I start feeding weekly with Phostrogen when the first flowers show colour.

There is some argument as to whether the plants should be stopped or not, at the six-leaf stage. I have tried both ways and I can see no advantage in stopping. Unstopped plants flower and fruit earlier and bear just as many peppers as the stopped ones. I have also found that syringing the plants with tepid water in the evenings greatly assists them to set. I also pick the peppers before they start to turn red. Left to ripen the unpicked fruits tend to inhibit further setting and fruiting.

Good varieties: Canape (an F_1 hybrid), New Ace (an F_1 hybrid)
Pests and/or diseases: aphids, slugs and snails, caterpillars
Blanching time: 3 minutes

Exhibition points:	Condition	8
(fruits should be plump, well	Colour	3
coloured, firm and fresh)	Uniformity	4
		15

Cardoon

The cardoon is closely related to the globe artichoke and resembles it in many ways. It is a large plant and needs to be spaced 1.2 metres (4 ft) apart each way to allow room for full development. Seeds are sown in a frame or under cloches in April or May, one seed to each 7-cm (3-in.) pot. Ground preparation involves digging a trench 45 cm (1½ ft) deep and throwing in a good, thick layer of manure. Put the seedlings out into their cropping positions when they are large enough, and make sure they never go short of water. Stake the plants and in early October tie the stems loosely together and surround them with brown paper to blanch them. Then earth them up and they will be ready for the table in November.

The leaf ribs of cardoons cook to a nice, nutty flavour and the flower heads are cooked and served much in the same way as globe artichokes.

Good variety: Improved White
Pests and/or diseases: usually trouble-free

Exhibition points:	Condition	4
(heads should be firm, clean and	Size	3
well-blanched)	Solidity	4
	Uniformity	4
		15

Carrot (root crop group)

Carrot varieties differ in the length and shape of their edible roots. The long, tapering varieties can attain a length of 90 cm (3 ft) and more in the exhibitor's bed, but they are not the ideal for shallow, stony soils. For soils of medium depth,

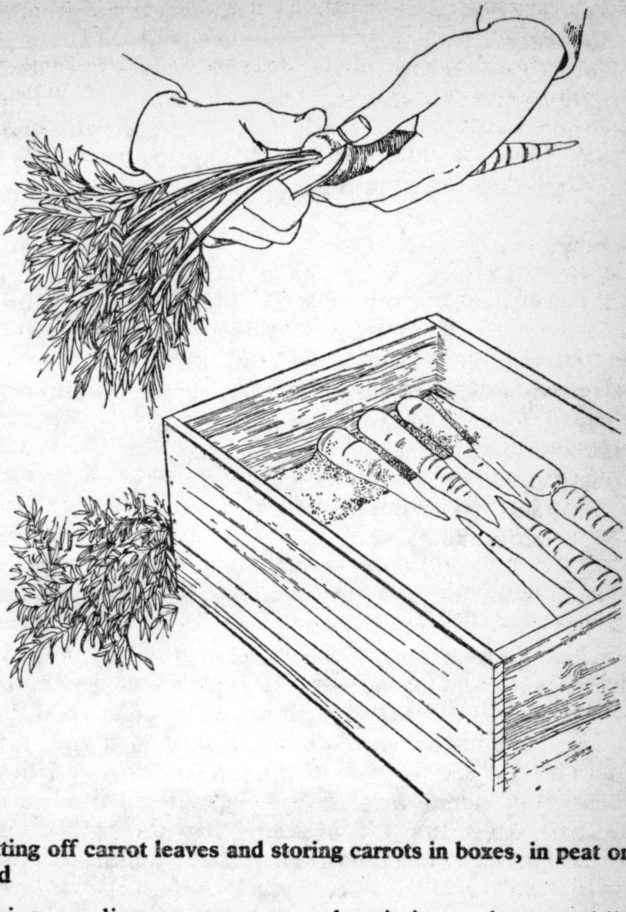

Cutting off carrot leaves and storing carrots in boxes, in peat or sand

the intermediate or stump-rooted varieties are better, while on very shallow soils only the globe varieties do well. The soil should be fertile and preferably manured for a previous crop; carrot roots tend to fork in freshly manured ground.

Seeds are sown successionally from March to July, starting the earliest sowings under cloches. Sow thinly in rows 20 cm (9 in.) apart and leave the seedlings unthinned until the thinnings are about 7 cm (3 in.) long and large enough for use in salads and for cooking. Roots remaining in the ground in October are lifted, cleaned of soil and stored in sand or peat for winter use. In areas where carrot fly is very troublesome despite insecticidal treatments, late June sowings will escape attention, as the pest has finished laying its first batch of eggs by then. It lays a second batch in August, by which time the carrots are big enough to cope with the problem.

Good varieties:
  Long tapering roots – St Valery
  Stump-rooted – Autumn King, Pioneer (an F_1 hybrid), Chantenay Red Cored
  Globe-rooted – Planet (an F_1 hybrid)
Pests and/or diseases: carrot fly, small rodents, wireworm
Blanching time: 2 to 4 minutes

Exhibition points:	Condition	5
(roots should be shapely, of good	Form	3
deep colour, tender and free of	Colour	6
small, fibrous roots)	Uniformity	6
		20

Cauliflower (brassica group)
Good cauliflowers are not as difficult to grow as some people claim. Gardeners who achieve curds no bigger than button-holes have deprived their 'caulies' of one or more of three essential soil ingredients – humus, plant food and water. Cauliflowers need all three in liberal amounts. More than any other crop, cauliflowers need to be watered daily in dry weather, not with a watering can, but with a sprinkler left running for 20 to 30 minutes. There is also some substance in the old gardener's tale of cutting a 2-cm (1-in.) long length-wise slit, halfway down the stem, just before the curd begins to form and sticking a matchstick in it to keep it open. For some reason the curd grows faster and better for this apparent mutilation.

Cauliflowers, like carrots, come in varieties that mature at different times of the year, if they are sown at the right time. By choosing early, mid-season and late varieties it is possible to enjoy tip-top curds from June to March. One of the problems with 'caulies' is that all the plants in the row are ready for eating at the same time, and, unless they are cut, some will run to seed and will be unusable. To prevent this, cut them in peak condition and hang the surplus upside down in a cool, airy place until you want them.

For the earliest crops, sow the seeds in warmth in February and March. Seeds may also be sown singly in 7-cm (3-in.) pots in September and the seedlings overwintered in a cold greenhouse or frame for planting out in March. For summer and autumn cropping, seeds of the appropriate varieties are sown, in a seed bed, from March to May and the young plants planted out 45 cm (1½ ft) apart when they are ready.

Good varieties:
- Early – Forerunner, Early Snowball
- Mid-season – Dominant, Rocket
- Late – Canberra, White Heart
- Winter – Snow's Winter White, St George

Pests and/or diseases: caterpillars, root fly, club root, white fly
Blanching time: 3 minutes

Exhibition points: (curds should be light, pure white and free from staining)		
	Condition	10
	Solidity	6
	Uniformity	4
		20

Celeriac

Celeriac is the answer for the gardener who can't be bothered to dig trenches for celery. Celeriac has a swollen root that keeps in good condition for several weeks after it matures and it has a good flavour closely resembling the more common celery. It is ready for lifting in October and November from the ground, although in areas subject to cold winters it is advisable to lift and store the roots in boxes of sand or peat in a dry, frost-free place. In the southern half of the country, in normal winters, it is enough just to earth them up or cover them with cloches.

Seeds are sown in warmth in March and the plants put out in late May or early June, in rows 30 cm (1 ft) apart, with 30 cm

(1 ft) between plants in the rows. Celeriac likes a fertile, moist soil and responds to weekly feeds of liquid fertilizer from the end of June to the end of August.

Good varieties: Erfurt, Marble Ball
Pests and/or diseases: leaf spot, celery fly

Exhibition points:	Condition	7
(roots should be smooth, of medium	Form	4
size and good depth)	Uniformity	4
		15

Celery
There are two distinct types of celery, both of which are equally delicious whether eaten raw or cooked. They differ in the extent of cultivation necessary to produce good crisp 'sticks'.

Self-blanching or American celery
This variety does not need blanching and therefore does not require the deep trenching required by the other celery varieties. It is not hardy so is should be harvested before the autumn frosts come along and ruin it. Seeds are sown in March, in a temperature of 18°C (65°F). The seedlings are pricked out, grown on and planted out 30 cm (12 in.) apart each way, when all risk of frost is over.

Blanching celery
Thorough soil preparation is necessary to grow good crops of crisp, long-stemmed celery. In winter dig a trench 60 cm (2 ft) deep and 45 cm (1½ ft) wide. Into the bottom of the trench, put a foot deep layer of rotted manure or compost, then replace some of the excavated soil until the level of the trench is about 15 cm (6 in.) below the surrounding soil. Leave the soil to settle and tidy up the remaining soil on both sides of the trench so that it may be used to grow catch crops such as lettuce.

Seed is sown in March, in a temperature of 18°C (65°F) and the plants put out in early June, after hardening off. Plant them 20 cm (9 in.) apart along the centre of the trench and finish off by flooding the trench with water. Celery is really a bog plant and needs a lot of water at its roots at all stages of growth. Blanching begins in early August and involves earthing up the stems in stages. Hold the stems close together in one hand and draw soil up to them with a trowel held in the other hand, until the soil is almost touching the lower leaves. Some gardeners wrap the stems in corrugated cardboard, or drop drainpipes over them before earthing-up begins. This is to prevent soil getting down between the stems and to keep slugs at bay. Earth up twice more at three-week intervals, as the plants grow, until you end with a filled-in ridged trench shaped like an elongated, inverted V. Celery will not withstand frost and needs covering with straw or ventilated polythene sheets for protection.

Good varieties:
  Self-blanching – American Green, Golden Self-blanching
  Blanching – Giant White, Giant Pink
Pests and/or diseases: leaf spot, celery fly
Blanching time: 3 minutes
Exhibition points:
(stalks should be firm, long, clean and well blanched, there should be no flower stems in the centres of the heads)

Condition	7
Size	4
Solidity	5
Uniformity	4
	20

Chicory

Chicory is the vegetable that produces those delicious, white, torpedo-shaped 'chicons', so delectable in winter salads. Seeds are sown outdoors, in drills 30 cm (1 ft) apart at any time from mid-April to the end of June. As soon as they are large enough, thin the seedlings to 20 cm (9 in.) apart. Keep them growing, and, by late October or early November, the plants will be ready for forcing and blanching. Chicory must be blanched, otherwise the chicons taste bitter if they are yellowish-green in colour.

Indoor forcing

Lift the roots and trim them to 20 cm (8 in.) in length and cut the leaves back to within 1 cm (½ in.) of the crown. Place the roots upright in deep pots or boxes of moist sand so that their tips are just covered, and put them in a warm, totally dark place. The chicons will emerge and be ready for eating in about three to four weeks' time.

Outdoor forcing

Cut all the leaves right back to the crown in October or early November and draw a 20-cm (8-in.) depth of soil over the crowns. The tips of the new growth, the chicons, will peep through the soil from January onwards. When the tips appear the chicons are ready for eating. They can be forced into earlier maturity by covering all or part of the row with cloches in November, after cutting back the leaves.

Good varieties: Witloof or Large Brussels, Winter Fare (eaten green without blanching)
Pests and/or diseases: aphids
Blanching time: 2 minutes

Exhibition points:	Condition	4
(chicons should be long, solid, crisp,	Length	4
tender and well blanched)	Blanching	4
	Uniformity	3
		15

Cress

There are three kinds of cress – ordinary curled cress, American or land cress and watercress. All may be grown from seeds.

Curled cress

Contrary to normal practice, our aim here is to produce long, drawn seedlings which are eaten at the cotyledon leaf stage, i.e. when the seed leaves have unfolded. The easiest way to grow curled cress is to sow the seeds (at any time of the year) on to moist blotting paper, flannel, or any absorbent material. The container is kept in a warm, fairly dark place and the seeds will germinate quickly. They are ready to eat when they are about 2 to 5 cm (1 to 2 in.) tall. Growing cress in this way interests children and is a good way to get them involved in gardening at an early age.

Cress can also be grown in shallow trays containing a 7-cm (3-in.) depth of seed compost. Sow the seeds fairly thickly on the surface of the compost, water them and place a sheet of black polythene over them. Leave them until the seedlings are touching the polythene, then remove the latter, allow the plants 24 hours to 'green' and then cut at soil level with scissors.

Cress and mustard go together like eggs and bacon. If you want both to be ready for eating at the same time, sow the cress three days before the mustard.

Good varieties: Extra Curled, Super Salad.
Pests and/or diseases: usually trouble-free

American or land cress
Although it looks and tastes very much like watercress, land cress does not need as much water at its roots. At the same time it does require a soil that is always moist, otherwise its leaves are tough and tasteless. If you have a partially shaded, damp area of soil in the garden sow it with land cress and it will thrive for many years. As it is a perennial sow the seeds in August where you want to grow it. Sow thinly and shallowly and thin the seedlings to 15 cm (6 in.) apart. Keep the bed free of weeds and water well during dry spells. There is only one variety and it is usually untroubled by pests and diseases.

Watercress
Although watercress grows like a weed in and on the verges of fresh, running water, it is extremely difficult to grow in the garden. In fact, it is not really worth trying. It is far better to concentrate on growing good crops of land cress to be sure of an edible crop.

Cucumber
Many people have told me that they will not eat a cucumber, either because they find it tastes bitter or because it gives them a tummy-ache. They would suffer from neither complaint if they ate a properly grown cucumber fresh off the plant. The older a cucumber is before it is eaten the more bitter it tastes and the more likely it is to cause stomach

upsets. Bitterness may also result from incorrect cultivation. The older, traditional varieties of greenhouse cucumbers bear male and female flowers, and to prevent bitterness the male flowers should be pinched off before they open and before they can pollinate the females. The more modern varieties bear female flowers only and the problem does not, therefore, arise. For some reason, cucumbers are also more likely to taste bitter when they are grown on a single main stem, or leader. I stop my plants when they have grown four leaves and grow two laterals on for fruiting and I never get bitter fruit.

Greenhouse cultivation

Providing their cultural needs are understood and met, cucumbers are prolific croppers. You should get upwards of twenty fruits from a single plant. Their first requirement is a fertile soil which never dries out, but which is, at the same time, well-drained. In badly drained soils the flowers either fail to set or, if they do, the fruits turn yellow and drop off before they begin to develop.

There are two ways of achieving ideal root conditions. The first is to cut a number of 30-cm (1-ft) square turves and build them into a 20-cm (9-in.) high, hollow rectangle on the greenhouse bed. The central empty area should be about 20 cm (9 in.) square and the turves are laid face downwards. The hollow is half-filled with a 50:50 mixture of soil and well-rotted farmyard manure and the seedling cucumber is planted in it. As the plant grows it is liberally watered and the hollow is topped up with a similar soil-manure mixture until it almost reaches the top. Each plant is stopped at four leaves and the two emerging lateral growths are trained and tied to a supporting framework of canes or led along each side of the greenhouse ridge. Weekly feeding with a liquid fertilizer begins six weeks after planting.

The second growing method is to put each plant into a bottomless ring standing on a soil or gravel bed. The soil mixture and growing system are identical to that suggested for cultivation in turves. Further information on bottomless rings will be found under tomato cultivation (*see* p. 134).

Seeds are sown singly in 7-cm (3-in.) pots in March, by pushing them edge-on into the compost which these pots contain. They are more prone to rot if they are sown flat-sides down. To be sure of good germination, a steady temperature of around 18°C (65°F) is necessary.

As well as plenty of water, most greenhouse varieties grow best in a warm, humid atmosphere, conditions that do not suit tomatoes and other crops. So, if you are growing a cucumber plant in a cool greenhouse with other crops, choose a suitable variety such as Conqueror and plant it at the furthest point away from the door and draughts.

Outdoor cultivation – ridge cucumbers

There are a few cucumber varieties that are suitable for outdoor cultivation. The fruits are shorter and thicker than the greenhouse varieties and their skins are dotted with 'pimple' growths. When they are cut young, they are as tasty and succulent as the more traditional, indoor kinds.

Seeds are sown singly in 7-cm (3-in.) pots, in a temperature of 18°C (65°F) in late March and April. Ground preparation involves digging a hole 45 cm (1½ ft) deep and 60 cm (2 ft) square, with 60 cm (2 ft) between the holes. Into each hole put a bucketful of rotted manure or compost, fill up with soil and firm it down. When the job is done, the surface level of the hole should be about 15 cm (6 in.) above the surrounding soil. When the plants are ready and there is no more likelihood of frost, put them, one per ridge, above each hole. Water well and stop each plant when it has made six leaves to encourage it to produce fruiting laterals. Feeding with liquid fertilizer starts when the first cucumber has set and is beginning to grow. The fruits are ready for cutting when they are about 20 cm (9 in.) long and before they start yellowing at their ends.

Gherkins and pickling cucumbers are grown in the same way as ridge or outdoor cucumbers.

Good varieties:

Greenhouse – Conqueror, Bittex (an F_1 hybrid), Pepinex '69 (an F_1 hybrid, all female flowers)

Outdoor or ridge – Burpee Hybrid (an F_1 hybrid), Greenline

Gherkin – Prolific

Pests and/or diseases: aphids, grey mould, mildew

Exhibition points:	Condition	10
(fruits should be long, unmarked,	Form	4
young and straight with short necks	Uniformity	4
and with remains of flowers still evident)		18

Endive

Endive is a salad vegetable in demand in the autumn and winter when lettuces are scarce and expensive. Seeds are sown in June or July, in rows 30 cm (1 ft) apart and the seedlings thinned to 38 cm (15 in.) apart. Endive needs plenty of water during dry weather and an occasional liquid feed in August to speed growth. When eaten green, endive is unpalatably bitter and needs blanching to bring out its flavour. Bearing in mind that the blanching process takes six weeks, select the number of plants you will require and start blanching six weeks before you want them for eating.

Blanching may be done in a number of ways. When the leaves are completely dry, you can draw them together and tie them loosely with twine or raffia or you can cover the chosen plants with inverted flower pots, placing stones over the drainage holes to exclude light. Thirdly, you can place one or more cloches, complete with end-pieces, over the selected plants and cover them with a sheet of black polythene.

Good variety: Batavian Broad-Leaved

Pests and/or diseases: aphids, slugs

Exhibitions points:	Condition	6
(heads should be crisp, tender,	Blanching	5
well blanched and clean)	Uniformity	4
		15

Kohl rabi (brassica group)

Kohl rabi is also called turnip cabbage because it belongs to the cabbage family and it tastes something like a cross between a cabbage and a turnip. It grows a round, edible root about the size of a cricket ball and it may be green- or purple-skinned depending on the variety. Seeds are sown in April and May in rows 30 cm (12 in.) apart, and the seedlings are thinned to 20 cm (9 in.) apart. Kohl rabi appreciates a deep, fertile soil and plenty of moisture at the roots. Unless it is watered in dry spells the roots become hard and woody and of little use in the kitchen.

Good varieties: Purple Vienna, White Vienna
Pests and/or diseases: club root, root fly
Blanching time: 1½ minutes (diced)

Exhibition points:	Condition	7
('roots' should be medium-sized,	Uniformity	5
tender, unmarked and small-leaved)		12

Leek (onion family)
Leeks are so hardy they will live through the hardest winters unscathed, provided their growth is not soft. For very early crops and for exhibition the seeds are sown in warmth in January and February and the seedlings planted out in April. For normal garden use seeds are sown in a seed bed in March. Growth, after germination, is very slow at first, but by May or June the young plants will be about 20 cm (9 in.) long and ready for planting out. Most of my leeks are planted as the early potatoes are lifted. The potato drills were well manured at planting time and all the soil now needs is a dusting of Growmore fertilizer, after it has been levelled and firmed.

Lift the leek plants carefully from the seed bed with a trowel, trying to keep their roots intact. There are two planting methods. The first involves making holes about 15 cm (6 in.) deep and 20 cm (9 in.) apart with a dibber and dropping a leek into each one. Instead of replacing the soil the hole is filled with water which 'puddles' the plant into place. Personally, I prefer to plant in the usual way, with a trowel, leaving about 5 to 7 cm (2 to 3 in.) of each plant showing above the soil. I find that they grow away quicker this way than by puddling them in. Allow 45 cm (1½ ft) between the rows. As the plants grow they are earthed up to

Blanching collars on leeks

secure a good length of blanched stem. When earthing, try not to get soil down between the leaves, as this can cause rotting. Some gardeners place cardboard collars around the leeks before earthing and others blanch using 60 to 90 cm (2 to 3 ft) long, 10 cm (4 in.) diameter, earthen drainpipes.

Good varieties: Musselburgh, Catalina
Pests and/or diseases: white tip, rust
Blanching time: 1 minute

Exhibition points:	Condition	8
(stems should be long, thick and well	Solidity	8
blanched and show no tendency to	Uniformity	4
bulbing above the roots)		20

Lettuce
A good, crisp lettuce is the basic ingredient of all summer salads. With care, planning and careful choice of varieties, it is

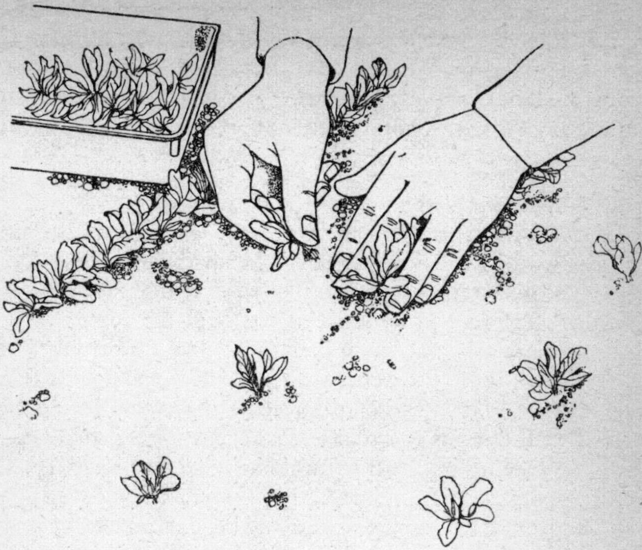

Thinning lettuces

possible to have fresh lettuce from the garden or greenhouse for the greater part of the year.

Summer lettuce

Begin by digging plenty of well-rotted manure or compost into the soil in winter. Lettuces are hungry plants and yield poor, loose hearts in soil that is low in humus and plant foods. I make my first sowing under cloches in early March, using a variety such as All The Year Round, and I never sow a row more than 1.8 to 2.4 metres (6 to 8 ft) in length at any one time. Our aim is to produce a continuous supply of lettuces throughout the summer, rather than a wasteful glut for a short period.

The seedlings under the cloches are thinned to 30 cm (12 in.) apart and the thinnings thrown on the compost heap. It is just not worth transplanting lettuce, they never do as well as undisturbed seedlings and anyway there are more seeds in the packet than anyone can possibly need. Two weeks after thinning, i.e. about the end of March, I sow a further short row and continue to repeat the process until August. In addition to an adequate supply of nutrients, lettuces, being very leafy plants, must have a moist soil during growth. Put the sprinkler on them as soon as the soil surface looks the least bit dry. Allow 20 to 30 cm (9 to 12 in.) between the rows.

Winter lettuces outdoors

I must stress that summer varieties are useless for autumn and winter sowings. Suitable varieties are sown from the end of August to mid-October, in soil that is reasonably fertile. No additional fertilizer is applied, as we want the plants to be hardy, with no soft growth for frost to damage. Sow thinly and thin the seedlings to 5 to 7 cm (2 to 3 in.) apart when four leaves have formed. To be sure of success, the rows should be covered with cloches to avoid losses through frost and snow. Leave the cloches in position until late March or early April, the timing depending on the weather. The moment the spring temperatures start rising, dust the soil between the rows with dried blood and hoe it into the top inch of soil. Whether you replace the cloches or not depends on how soon you want hearted lettuce. You can either leave the plants uncovered or they can stay under cloches until they are ready for cutting in April and May. Over the years I have tried many winter varieties and have been more pleased with Valdor than with any other.

Winter lettuce under glass

Here again only those varieties that are suitable will succeed and they must be sown at the right time. Given these conditions, good winter lettuce can be grown in cold or slightly heated greenhouses. They are, however, prone to fungus attack, at soil level, unless the soil is well drained and fairly dry on the surface. I find it pays to grow the plants on slightly raised ridges, about an inch above the general bed level. The extra drainage keeps them dry around the collar and they remain healthy. Sow the seeds *in situ* at the right time to suit the variety and thin to 30 cm (12 in.) apart at the four-leaf stage. Go easy with the watering and give a touch of ventilation on sunny days.

Lettuce types are in four main groups:

1. Butterhead varieties (B), with soft leaves and rather loose hearts.
2. Crisphead varieties (C), with serrated, brittle leaves and tight hearts.
3. Cos varieties (Co), with upright leaves that are tied and blanched.
4. Loose leaf varieties (L), these being plants to leave in the ground so that a few leaves can be cut as required.

Good varieties:

Summer lettuce – All The Year Round (B), Fortune (B), Webbs Wonderful (C), Minetto (C), Suzan (B), Tom Thumb (C)

Winter lettuce, outdoors – Arctic King (B), Valdor (B), Winter Density (Co)

Winter lettuce, greenhouse – Kloek (B), sow August or November; Kweick (B), sow late August or early September; Magida (B), sow October–November

Pests and/or diseases: grey mould, aphids

Exhibition points:	Condition	6
(firm, blanched hearts and few,	Size and	
crisp, clean unbroken outer leaves)	firmness	5
	Uniformity	4
		15

Marrows

The best marrows for eating are not the monsters that adorn the altars of our churches at harvest festival. They are tough, tasteless and full of seeds. The fruits of the large bush and trailing marrows are at their best when they are about 30 cm (12 in.) long and those of the courgette type when they are 15 to 20 cm (6 to 8 in.) long.

Seeds of all the varieties may be sown outdoors, or in warmth, under cover. Sow in the greenhouse, or propagator, in April, sowing one seed on its edge to each 3-in. pot. Grow them on, harden them off and plant out in early June when there is no further risk of frost. For sowing outdoors wait until mid-May, then sow two seeds per 'station' and cover them with an inverted jam jar. If both seeds germinate, discard the weakest seedling and grow the strongest on. Keep the jam jar in position until the marrow plant gets too big for it.

Good and thorough ground preparation for marrows is really worthwhile. The best method is to dig a hole for each individual plant, spacing them 1.5 metres (5 ft) apart for trailing varieties and 1 metre (3 ft) apart for bush varieties. Dig each hole 45 to 60 cm (1½ to 2 ft) deep, 60 cm (2 ft) square. Into the bottom of the holes put a 30-cm (1-ft) deep layer of fresh manure or compost mixed with green lawn mowings from a lawn that has not been treated with weedkiller for 12 months. Before replacing the soil, sprinkle in a good handful of dried blood, then fill the hole and firm it down. A week before sowing or planting, fork a handful of blood, fish and bone into the top 5 to 7 cm (3 to 4 in.) of the soil in the holes. This is a rich diet, but you will be rewarded by an ample supply of marrows. Keep the plants well watered at all stages of growth.

I have also grown courgette marrows very successfully in growing bags, with two plants to each large bag. As the roots are confined, I start feeding every five to seven days with Phostrogen, as soon as the first fruit forms. As the plants have very large leaves, they may need as much as 9 litres (2 gallons) of water on warm, sunny days and at least half this amount a day at other times.

It may be necessary to assist in flower pollination although insects will often do the job very successfully. But, to be sure of pollination, take a male flower, strip off the petals and push its pollen-bearing core into the centre of the female flower. The females are easily recognized because they each have a tiny marrow tucked behind the petals. It often happens that all the first flowers are male. Don't worry, female flowers will appear in due course.

Good varieties:
  Trailing – Golden Delicious, Long White Trailing
  Bush – All Green Bush, Butternut, White Bush
  Courgette – Zucchini, Golden Zucchini
Pests and/or diseases: mildew
Blanching time: 3 minutes (cubed)

Exhibition points: (fruits should be young, firm and of good shape)	Condition	6
	Uniformity	4
		10

Melon

Contrary to common belief it is quite easy to grow good, juicy melons. All you need is a greenhouse, a frame or just a few cloches, if you choose the right varieties. For cloche cultivation the best is the F_1 hybrid Sweetheart.

Seeds are sown in April, two to a 7-cm (3-in.) pot, in a steady 21°C (70°F) temperature. If both seedlings come up, remove the weakest and cultivate the strongest.

When growing melons outdoors in frames or cloches, keep the cover on the frame and place the cloches in position a good two weeks before planting. This is done to warm up the soil ready to receive the plants and to prevent them being checked by coming from a warm greenhouse into cold soil.

When the plants have grown five leaves pinch out their growing points. There are both male and female flowers on the same plant, the females being recognized by having small swellings behind their petals. They have to be cross-pollinated by hand, using a soft brush or a small piece of cotton wool. Take the pollen from the male organs (anthers) and transfer it to the female organ (the stigma) in the centre of the flower. Keep the plants well watered, but reduce watering as the fruits begin to ripen. Overwatering at this stage impairs the flavour of the fruit. You can tell when the fruit is ripe when the end furthest from the stalk feels soft under gentle thumb pressure.

Good varieties:
  Greenhouse – Blenheim Orange
  Outdoor – Ogen, Sweetheart

Pests and/or diseases: cucumber mosaic

Exhibition points: (fruits should be large, ripe with a thin rind, flesh thick, juicy and of good, sweet flavour)	Condition	5
	Appearance	5
	Size	5
	Flavour	5
		20

Mushroom

Of all vegetables, I would rate the mushroom as the most difficult to grow successfully. The time-honoured method of cultivation involves getting hold of strawy horse manure, preferably from racing stables. Stack the manure into a heap about 1.8 metres (6 ft) high and about 1.2 × 1.2 metres (4 × 4 ft) in area, soaking it with water as you stack. Decomposition is rapid and after seven days the heap is turned and restacked. The whole process is repeated, three or four times, until the manure is a dark-brown, friable compost. The compost is placed in 20-cm (8-in.) deep boxes and the mushroom spawn inserted and firmed in. After ten days, a network of fine threads will appear on the compost surface.

This is the mycelium that will eventually yield mushrooms. Cover the mycelium with a 1-in. deep layer of a mixture of 4 parts peat, 1 part sand and 1 part chalk. Good garden soil may be used instead of the mixture, but it must be sterilized first. Keep the compost moist but not wet, and gather the mushrooms at or just after the button stage. During the growing period the temperature must be kept at a critical level – between 10°C and 18°C (50°F and 65°F).

Mushroom spawn may also be sown outdoors from April to August with, I fear, little chance of success. Sometimes it works, most times it doesn't. To sow, lift 60-cm (2-ft) squares of lawn or field turf about 2 cm (1 in.) thick, loosen the soil below and mix in a couple of handfuls of rotted 'organic'. Put a few mushroom spawn grains on top, replace the turves and firm them down.

By far the easiest and surest way of growing mushrooms is to use the prepared packs, that are readily available in garden centres and shops. Provided the growing instructions are followed you are certain of a worthwhile crop of delicious mushrooms.

Good buys: Darlington's Mushroom Spawn, Tubby Mushroom Pack

Pests and/or diseases: flies and aphids, fungi

Exhibition points: (they should be plump and rounded with the edges unbroken and with the gills, when visible, pink or pinkish-brown)	Condition	6
	Solidity	4
	Uniformity	2
		12

Mustard

Mustard seedlings for salads and sandwiches are grown in exactly the same way as cress (*see* p. 100).

Onion

There are several kinds of onions, all of which are easily grown and play an important role in a healthy and tasteful diet. Of all the kinds, the keeping-onions are the most commonly cultivated and the most valuable in the kitchen. They may be grown from two sources – from seeds and from sets.

Keeping-onions from sets

Onion sets are small onions in a state of arrested development. Commercial growers on the Continent sow seeds late in the season and harvest the small bulbs or sets in the autumn. They are stored over-winter under controlled conditions and are available through seed catalogues and shops from December onwards.

Although onions are hardy I find that it does not do to plant the sets outdoors too early. Frost does not destroy them, but they suffer such a severe growth check that the crop weight is adversely affected and many may run to seed. They may, of course, be planted in February if they are covered with cloches for protection. But my best crops come from sets planted in the open ground from late March to early April, when the weather is conducive to quick rooting and rapid leaf growth. To plant draw out shallow drills 20 to 30 cm (9 to 12 in.) apart and place the sets 20 cm (9 in.) apart in the drills. Don't push the sets down into the soil or they tend to be thrust upwards when their emerging roots meet the hard pad of soil underneath. It is better to draw soil around them and to firm them in from the sides. Also, cut away any long 'tails' of dry leaf stalks still adhering to the little bulbs. After planting, the tips of the sets should be just peeping above the soil.

Keeping-onions from seeds

The champion onion growers raise bulbs that weigh between 2.7 and 3 kg (6 and 7 lb) each. They achieve these beauties as a result of experience, expertise and some very special seeds. The seeds they use are the outcome of many years of selecting the biggest and best onions and growing them on to produce seeds in their second year. They also sow them very early, usually in late December or early January under glass, then pot the seedlings singly into 7- or 12-cm (3- or 5-in.) pots and plant them out in mid-April, in a very fertile bed. Seeds may also be sown in the seed bed in March and the seedlings transplanted when they are 10 to 15 cm (4 to 6 in.) tall. Outdoor sowings may be made even earlier by making use of cloches.

For most of us onions up to half a kilo in weight are quite big enough, but even to get these it pays to prepare the soil really well in winter. The best way is to remove the top soil from the onion bed to a depth of 30 cm (12 in.) and line the bottom with a 15-cm (6-in.) layer of fresh manure. Add 56 grams (2 oz) of bone meal per square metre, replace the soil and leave it to settle naturally. Then about two weeks before planting (either seedlings or sets) dust the bed with 'Blood, Fish and Bone', again at 56 grams (2 oz) to the square metre. Use a trowel to plant the seedlings and plant them at a depth which will avoid them toppling.

Keep the bed watered in dry weather and weed regularly by hand. Onions are shallow rooters and hoeing them disturbs their roots and reduces the crop. From the time they are planted until early June the onions concentrate on leaf growth, and the amount of leaf they make largely determines the size of the final bulbs. From early June leaf growth stops and food begins to flow down into the swelling bulbs. From this time onwards the onion bed should not have any additional feeding. When you see the bulbs beginning to swell, scrape some of the soil away from around them to make bulbing easier but be careful not to disturb their roots.

Harvesting and storing

As the plants reach maturity the leaves begin to lose their colour and flop over. At this stage (sometime in August) put a fork into the soil and gently lever the bulbs up about 2 or 3 in. without removing them from the soil. This loosens their roots and hastens ripening. About 10 to 14 days later lift the plants and lay them on their sides on the soil, with their roots facing the sun. To complete the ripening process the plants may be placed on the greenhouse staging, on sacks, or on wire-netting frames until their leaves are totally brown and dry. The best way to store them is to put them either in boxes or in the legs of old, laddered stocking-tights, leaving them in a cool, dry and airy place. They may also be strung in 'ropes', hung and used as required. Whatever method you use, inspect them frequently and remove any that show signs of mould before it spreads to other healthy bulbs.

Good varieties:
From sets – Stuttgart Giant, Sturon
From seeds – Ailsa Craig, Rijnsburger, Hygro, Superba (an F_1 hybrid)
Pests and/or diseases: onion fly, neck rot, white rot
Blanching time: 2 minutes (chopped)

Exhibition points:	Condition	5
(bulbs should be large, firm,	Size	5
thin-necked with unbroken skins)	Form	5
	Uniformity	5
		20

Autumn sowing
A few European onion varieties may be sown outdoors in the autumn to yield earlier crops. The seedlings are left unthinned in the seed bed and are transplanted to their final positions in April. In most areas cloche protection is advisable during the coldest months. There are also a number of Japanese onion varieties that are winter-hardy in the open. Their seeds are sown in August and the first of the crop is ready for the pot in the following June, a good month earlier than the European onions.

Suitable varieties:
European – Ailsa Craig, Autumn Queen
Japanese – Imai Early Yellow, Express Yellow (an F_1 hybrid)

Pickling onion
Pickling onions are small and thin-skinned and they are grown for preserving rather than for dry-storing. Seeds are sown outdoors in March and April, in rows 15 cm (6 in.) apart and the seedlings are left unthinned. The bulbs are ready for lifting by late July or early August. Lift them and dry them in the same way as I have described for keeping-onions.

Good variety: The Queen

Welsh onion
The Welsh onion is a perennial that will crop for several years. Seeds are sown in a seed bed in March and the seedlings planted out 20 cm (9 in.) apart when they are about 15 cm (6 in.) tall. Each plant grows a cluster of leaf bases and these are dug up and used as spring onions. To perpetuate the plants, leave a clump or two uncropped until the autumn, then lift, divide and replant the several off-sets.

Good variety: Ciboule

Spring onion
Seeds of the ordinary spring onion variety are sown, in succession, at regular intervals from March to August. They are sown fairly thickly and the seedlings are left unthinned to be pulled and chopped for salads as required. Seeds of the winter-hardy variety are sown in September, the young plants being ready for eating in the early spring.

Good varieties: White Lisbon, White Lisbon Winter Hardy

Tree onion
The tree onion is a perennial with long, tall stems bearing clusters of small 'cocktail' onions at the top. Seeds of this variety are unobtainable and the only way to procure it is to beg a few of the small bulblets from some gardener who happens to have them for planting in the autumn.

Japanese bunching onion
Seeds are sown in April and the plants are left to grow

untouched until they reach usable size in the second year. The Japanese bunching onion does not form a bulb and its large leaves, which remain green through the winter, are cut and chopped into salads.

Parsley

There are two distinct types of parsley (curled and Hamburg), which are different in appearance and in their use in the kitchen.

Curled parsley

Because it is sometimes difficult to germinate, parsley has gathered to itself a host of superstitions. Some sow it when the moon is full, others when it is new and yet others believe that it will only succeed if sown by a virtuous maiden. It is all non-sense. Parsley will germinate like any other vegetable, if its seeds find the conditions right. The main problem is the seed coat, which is unusually hard and impermeable. So, soak the seeds in tepid water for a day before sowing to soften their coats. Another method often used is to sow the seeds and then pour a kettle of boiling water over them before closing the drill.

My own sowing method varies with the time of year. In February or early March I sow very thinly in a seed tray in a propagator. Half the seedlings are planted out 20 cm (9 in.) apart in April and form a pretty edging to the herb border. The other half stay in the tray and are used for flavouring until the outdoor ones are ready. For winter use I make a sowing out-doors in August when germination is never a problem. I sow thinly, leave the row unthinned and cover it with cloches as soon as hard weather sets in. The spring and autumn sowings ensure that we have a constant source of fresh parsley for our sauces and garnishings. It is worth remembering that as parsley is closely related to the carrot it can be attacked by carrot fly and suitable precautions should be taken.

Good varieties: Bravour, Moss Curled
Pests and/or diseases: carrot fly

Exhibition points: Condition 5
(leaves should be fresh and of good colour)

Hamburg parsley
Hamburg parsley grows an edible root that is long and tapering like a parsnip's. Seeds are sown in March and April, in drills 30 cm (12 in.) apart and the seedlings are thinned to 15 cm (6 in.) apart. The roots are ready for use in September and may either be earthed up and left in the ground or they may be lifted and stored in boxes of sand or peat.

Good variety: Hamburg Turnip Rooted

Parsnip (root crop group)
Parsnips are among the most valuable of winter vegetables, being so hardy that they can be left in the ground and lifted for use as required. They will remain undamaged in a deep-frozen soil and, in fact, taste better after frost than before it. They are unfortunately susceptible to a condition known as canker, that appears as a rusty-brown discoloration around the tops of the roots. The disease can progress to the stage when the roots rot in the ground. As far as I know there is no known cure. I have found that late-sown parsnips (sown in late April and May) are less likely to be troubled. It also pays to change the position of the parsnip bed every year, and a little lime in the soil also helps. There are one or two canker-resistant varieties, although seed of these is not always available in the catalogues.

Another characteristic of parsnips is that even good quality seed has a comparatively low germination rate – often no more than about 60 per cent. Therefore, it is advisable to use the 'station' method of sowing. Take out shallow drills 20 cm (9 in.) apart and sow three seeds each at stations spaced 15 to 20 cm (6 to 8 in.) apart. If more than one seed germinates, thin them to the strongest one.

Good varieties: Hollow Crown Improved, Tender and True, White Gem
Pests and/or diseases: canker
Blanching time: 2 minutes (diced)

Exhibition points: (roots should be long, broad-shouldered, shapely and clean)	Condition	6
	Size	4
	Form	4
	Colour	2
	Uniformity	4
		20

Pea (legume group)

There are few flavours to compare with the taste of fresh green peas from the garden. By sowing suitable varieties at the right time it is possible to gather young pods for several weeks of the year. Pea varieties are grouped under the headings early, second early and maincrop. The term 'early' signifies that a particular variety is ready for cropping in less time than it takes a second early or a maincrop variety to reach maturity. It does not mean that the variety has to be sown early in the season. An early variety may, in fact, be sown anytime from early spring to late summer and is the only one that is suitable for late sowing, because it will crop before the frosts damage it.

Using an early variety, I make my first sowing in late February or early March, under cloches. I take out a 5 cm (2 in.) deep, 30 cm (12 in.) wide trench in the normal way and sow the seeds, spacing them about 7 cm (3 in.) apart. Peas need supporting, and, as I live in the country, twiggy sticks are readily available in the hedgerows. The farmer's permission is, of course, sought before I take my chopper to them. The sticks are placed in position 30 to 45 cm (1 to 1½ ft) apart along each side of the row so that the peas can start climbing as soon as they emerge from the soil. If sticks are not available, wire-netting may be used instead. In some gardens mice are tempted to dig for the peas. They can be discouraged by soaking the seeds, before sowing, in a paste of red lead and paraffin. Another good preventive is to strew the trench with dry holly leaves or bits of gorse before closing it in. Birds are also partial to peas and have a habit of pecking the tops of the seedlings as they come through the soil. The only way to stop them is to cover the row with wire or nylon netting.

Following the first sowing, I make successional sowings at monthly intervals from April to July. For the later sowing I have found that Kelvedon Wonder gives the best results. It is ready for picking in about 75 days from sowing and it also shows resistance to mildew, a fungus disease that tends to affect late-sown peas. It is also one of the best flavoured of all peas and I am content to use it throughout the season especially as, being a drawf variety, it needs little staking.

Sowings may also be made in October and November, using a round-seeded variety such as Meteor or Feltham First. It is advisable to cloche the rows to protect the seedlings from hard weather, and the cloches can be left in position until growth begins in earnest in spring.

Good varieties:

Early – Kelvedon Wonder 60 cm (2 ft), Vitalis 76 cm (2½ ft), Little Marvel 45 cm (1½ ft), Gradus 1.2 metres (4 ft)

Second early – Hurst Green Shaft 76 cm (2½ ft), Jof 90 cm (3 ft), Early Onward 60 cm (2 ft)

Maincrop – Onward 90 cm (3 ft), Achievement 1.5 metres (5 ft), Alderman 1.8 metres (6 ft)

Other peas:

Asparagus pea 45 cm (1½ ft)

This is not a true pea, although its mode of growth is rather similar. The curious winged pods are cooked and eaten whole. Seeds are sown 15 cm (6 in.) apart in shallow trenches in April and May and the pods picked when about 5 cm (2 in.) long.

Sugar pea 90 cm (3 ft)

The pods of sugar peas are picked before or just as the tiny peas begin to form. They are topped and tailed and cooked whole. Seeds are sown from March to April.

Pea, petit pois 60 cm (2 ft)

'Petit pois' are in great demand in Continental kitchens. The peas are only about half the size of our popular British varieties, but what they lack in size they make up for in their sweet flavour. They should be picked young, cooked and shelled just before serving.

Supporting peas with twigs/wire/nylon netting

Snap pea 1.5 metres (5 ft)
The snap pea looks like any other, but instead of having peas in hollow pods they are in pods with wall-to-wall flesh. They are usually cooked and eaten whole, but, if preferred, the peas and pods can be cooked and served separately and they are really delicious. Seeds are sown from April to June in the usual way for ordinary pea varieties.

Pests and diseases of peas: pea moth, pea weevil, mice, birds
Blanching time: 1 minute

Exhibition points:	Condition	8
(pods should be long, young,	Size of pods	4
unmarked and well-filled with the	Fullness of pods	4
'bloom' intact)	Uniformity	4
		20

Potato (root crop group)
The potato is an integral part of the British diet and, although space-consuming, it must be included in every cropping plan. Potatoes flower and produce seeds which are contained in the small, green and round tomato-like growths, often

seen above the leaves. These seeds, if sown, will grow into potato plants, but they will not be true to varietal type and neither will they yield a worthwhile crop in the first year. It is the custom, therefore, to grow potatoes from sets that are usually and erroneously called 'seeds'.

Seed potatoes of named varieties are available from January onwards. As a rough guide 3 kg (7 lb) of 'seed' will contain, on average, between 45 and 50 tubers which, ideally, should be about the size of a chicken's egg. It is advisable to buy seed potatoes as early as possible so that they may be 'chitted' for a few weeks prior to planting. Chitting involves placing the seed potatoes, on end, in shallow boxes or seed trays with their 'eyes' facing upwards. The 'eyes' are shallow depressions from which the stems and leaves will eventually grow and they are usually found in greater numbers on the blunt ends of the tubers.

The chitted tubers are kept in a warm, light place for the purpose of prodding them into growth. After a period of a few weeks they will be covered with sturdy, purply-green shoots a few inches in length. When you are ready to plant them, rub off all but three or four of the strongest shoots. Seed potatoes that have been chitted come into bearing a week or two earlier than ones that are planted immediately after purchase. Also make sure when you buy your 'seed' that it is 'certified stock'. Potatoes are prone to virus attack and by buying certified seed you are guaranteed that it is free from disease. Lastly, before buying, decide whether you want early or maincrop varieties. Early varieties, as their name implies, are ready for cooking earlier than the maincrops and are eaten 'out of the ground' about 12 weeks after planting. Earlies do not keep well and if you want potatoes for lifting and storing you need the maincrop variety.

The best way to plant seed potatoes is to take out a trench 20 cm (8 in.) deep and about 30 cm (1 ft) wide. Into the bottom of the trench put a good 7- to 10-cm (3- to 4-in.) layer of manure or compost, and place the tubers on the organic material, 20 cm (9 in.) apart in the case of earlies and 30 cm (12 in.) apart for maincrop varieties. Close the soil back over them and firm it with the back of the spade. Early varieties are

Planting 'chitted' potatoes

planted from mid-March to mid-April and maincrop ones in April and early May.

When the potatoes are through the soil and growing there are two points to bear in mind. They are not hardy and can be severely damaged by frost. If frost is imminent either cover the leaves with soil, if they are not too tall, or place sheets of newspaper or polythene over them overnight. Furthermore, as they grow, draw soil from the sides of the rows, up around the stems. This helps to support them and it reduces the risk of some of the new potatoes being exposed on the soil surface and turning green. Green potatoes are poisonous and should never be eaten.

Maincrop potatoes are ready for lifting when the leaves shrivel and die back to soil level. To harvest, lift them with a fork, leave them to dry on the soil for an hour or two, clean the worst of the soil off them and bag them up in sacks or brown paper bags. Clear polythene bags are no use because they admit light. Store them in a cool, frost- and rodent-free shed or garage and they will keep for several months.

Earthing potatoes

Good varieties:

Earlies – Pentland Javelin, Arran Pilot, Home Guard, Ulster Chieftain, Sharpe's Express, Maris Peer

Maincrop – Majestic, King Edward, Pentland Dell, Desiree, Golden Wonder

Pests and/or diseases: eelworm, wireworm, blight, scab

Exhibition points: (the tubers should have few and shallow 'eyes' and have whole, clean and unmarked skins, they should also be according to schedule, i.e. round, oval or kidney-shaped)		
	Condition	4
	Size	4
	Shape	4
	Eyes	4
	Uniformity	4
		20

Pumpkin

Pumpkins can achieve considerable weights of over 90 kg (200 lb) each. Under normal cultivation they usually attain weights of between 13 and 18 kg (30 and 40 lb). Pumpkins are treated very much like marrows, their seeds being sown either indoors or outdoors. Sow them in warmth in April, one seed to a 7-cm (3-in.) pot. Plant the resulting plants out in early June, allowing 1.5 metres (5 ft) between each plant. Outdoors, sow in the middle of May, under cloches or jam jars. As with melons and marrows, the female flowers need to be hand-pollinated to ensure a good set. After pollination allow no more than three fruits to form on each plant, and remove all other flowers as soon as they appear. When the pumpkins are about 30 cm (12 in.) long, cut and use two of them and leave the other to grow.

Good varieties: Hundredweight, Mammoth
Pests and/or diseases: usually trouble-free

Exhibition points:	Condition	6
(fruit should be round and firm	Size	2
and evenly ripe)	Solidity	2
		10

Radish (root crop group)
Whether you wish to grow long- or round-rooted radish give them the best bit of ground in the vegetable garden. When they are well grown radishes are crunchy and delicious, but in poor ground they form small, stringy roots and often run to seed prematurely. Dig in plenty of well-rotted manure in the winter, and a week or so before sowing top-dress with a general fertilizer at 28 to 56 g (1 to 2 oz) to the square metre. It is equally important to keep the radish patch well watered in dry weather.

As the seeds are large enough to be handled individually, I sow them 7 cm (3 in.) apart and save the bother of thinning later on. My first sowing is made under cloches in February and I continue sowing at three- to four-week intervals right through to June. To save space, I sow short 60 to 90 cm (2 to 3 ft) long rows in between the ends of rows of other vegetables, such as onions, lettuce and peas. There are also radishes that can be sown in July and August, to provide winter flavouring. Their roots are shaped like short parsnips and are considerably larger than those of the summer radishes.

Seeds are sown in rows 15 cm (6 in.) apart and the seedlings thinned also to 15 cm (6 in.) apart. The roots may be left in the ground for use from October onwards, or they may be lifted and stored in boxes of peat or sand.

Good varieties:
Summer – Cherry Belle, French Breakfast, Sparkler
Winter – Black Spanish, China Rose, Mino Early
Pests and/or diseases: usually trouble-free

Exhibition points (summer radish): (roots should be fresh, firm, unmarked, of good colour and medium-sized, leaves should be short and intact)	Condition	6
	Size	2
	Uniformity	2
		10

Rhubarb

Rhubarb may be grown from seed or bought as young one-year-old plants. From seed, rhubarb takes two years before it is well enough established for cutting to begin. If roots are planted they should be left untouched for one whole season and only moderately cropped in the second. Once established, rhubarb may be 'forced' to give earlier than normal pickings. One way of forcing is to place an old upturned bucket with a hole in the bottom over the clump, after first covering it with a good, thick layer of strawy manure. The bucket affords protection and as there is little light, the stems are drawn towards the hole and are partially blanched and very sweet. Another way is to lift a clump or two in December or January and put them in soil in deep boxes and place them under the greenhouse staging. After lifting and forcing the clump is a spent force and is best discarded.

Once it is planted, rhubarb spends its whole life in the same place, so it pays to dig in plenty of manure or compost before planting. Every year, top-dress the bed with more 'organics', and, as an added boost, dust it over with dried blood in early March. Pull the sticks when they are young and succulent, but always leave a few to feed the roots. Stop pulling in June and wait for the second crop of new sticks that pop up in August. To grow from seeds sow them in a seed bed in March or April, and thin the resulting seedlings to 30 cm (12 in.) apart. Leave the young plants to develop and transplant them into their final positions when their leaves have died back in October or November.

Good varieties: Champagne, Victoria
Pests and/or diseases: usually trouble-free

Exhibition points: (sticks should be long, straight, thick, of good colour and they should snap cleanly)		
	Condition	4
	Length and straightness	2
	Colour	4
	Uniformity	2
		12

Salsify

Salsify is also called the vegetable oyster because its flavour is reminiscent of the shellfish. It is a winter vegetable. Seeds are sown outdoors in April and May in rows 38 cm (15 in.) apart and the resulting seedlings are thinned to 20 cm (9 in.) apart. The long roots are ready from October onwards, when they should be lifted and stored in boxes of peat or sand. On light, very well-drained soils the roots may be left in the ground and lifted and used as required.

Good variety: Sandwich Island
Pests and/or diseases: usually trouble-free

Shallots (onion group)

Shallots are grown from bulbs planted at any time from February onwards when the soil is dry enough to walk on. Plant them in the same way as onion sets in rows 20 cm (9 in.) apart, with 20 cm (9 in.) spacing between the bulbs in the rows. Shallots are usually used in two ways. They may be pulled young before new bulbs begin to form and when the leaves are green, for chopping into salads. Or they may be left to mature, and, when their leaves have died back, the bulbs are harvested and dried like onions. One shallot bulb will yield several more bulbs which are perfect for pickling in vinegar. For a very early crop of 'scallions' for salads plant the bulbs in January or February in boxes of good soil or compost in the greenhouse.

Good varieties: Dutch Yellow (yellow skinned), Hative de Niort (red skinned)
Pests and/or diseases: usually trouble-free

Exhibition points: (bulbs should be round with thin necks, unbroken skins and they should be firm; shallots for pickling should be small)	Condition	5
	Size	3
	Uniformity	4
		12

Spinach

Although not everyone's choice, spinach is a flavoursome and health-giving vegetable. By sowing the right kind, at the right time, spinach can be available practically throughout the year.

Summer spinach

Being a leafy vegetable, similar to lettuce, summer spinach needs similar soil conditions, i.e. a soil rich in organic material and plenty of water at the roots. In thin, dry soils it 'bolts' almost before it is ready for cutting. Seeds are sown 15 cm (6 in.) apart, in drills 30 cm (12 in.) apart from March until June to provide a succession of leaves for the table. Like beetroot the seeds are 'clustered', so thin the seedlings to one at each 'station' as soon as they are large enough to handle. When the plants have attained a reasonable height, thin them by using them. Lift every other plant as required and leave the others to grow on. When cropping fully grown plants, cut two or three leaves at a time from each one. The plants will then grow more leaves to replace the ones you have taken. The cropping period of a plant is about three weeks from the time the first leaves are cut.

Good varieties: Viking, Longstanding Round
Blanching time: 2 to 3 minutes

Exhibition points: (leaves should be thick, fresh, dark green and clean)	Condition	6
	Size and substance	4
	Uniformity	2
		12

Winter spinach

Winter spinach is very similar to the summer variety except that it is hardier and its season of use extends from November to April. Seeds are sown from July to September in drills 30 cm (12 in.) apart, and the resulting seedlings subsequently thinned to 15 cm (6 in.) apart. When cutting take only two or three of the largest leaves from each plant and during severe weather cover the plants with cloches to keep the crop clean and usable.

Good varieties: Broad-leaved Prickly, Greenmarket

New Zealand spinach
New Zealand spinach grows low on the ground and each plant needs an all-round spacing of 90 cm (3 ft) to allow for its full growth. Seeds are sown in warmth, in March and April, to provide plants for putting out in late May or early June. New Zealand spinach tolerates hot, dry conditions and is far less likely to run to seed than the ordinary summer spinach.

Good variety: New Zealand
Pests and/or diseases of spinach: downy mildew, leaf spot

Exhibition points:	Condition	8
(tips should be about 3 in. long and of	Uniformity	4
pencil-thickness, dark green in		12
colour)		

Swede (brassica group)
Although swedes are a root crop I have included them in the brassica group because, botanically, they are of the cabbage family and are, therefore, susceptible to the same pests and diseases. In view of this it is logical and advisable to group them with brassicas in any crop-rotation system.

Swedes are fairly hardy but they can be ruined by very severe frosts. In the milder parts of the country it is enough just to earth them over and leave them in the ground, but, if in doubt, lift the roots in October, remove the leaves and store them in sacks, in a cool and dry place. Seeds are sown in April and May in rows 45 to 60 cm (1½ to 2 ft) apart and the resulting seedlings are thinned to 45 cm (1½ ft) apart. Swedes are large, leafy plants so allow 60 cm (2 ft) between them and rows of other vegetables.

Good varieties: Acme, Marian
Pests and/or diseases: flea beetle, cabbage root fly, club root
Blanching time: 1 minute (diced)

Exhibition points: (roots should be solid, of good shape and with small taproots; skin should be clean and unmarked)	Condition	6
	Size and solidity	5
	Uniformity	4
		15

Sweet corn

Good crops of sweet corn are possible in our climate, provided the requirements of this exacting vegetable are understood and met. It is not hardy, yet it needs a long season of growth before it will yield fat, tasty cobs. It also hates root disturbance and seldom does well after transplanting. Seeds may be sown in two ways. The best method is to sow them singly in 7-cm (3-in.) peat pots, in warmth, in late March or early April. When the danger of frost is over, the plants, in their pots, are planted out 45 cm (1½ ft) apart all round. By using peat pots which soon disintegrate in the soil the plants suffer no root disturbance. Alternatively, the seeds may be sown *in situ* from the middle to the end of May under cloches, with the cloches being left in position until the plants are touching their tops.

Sweet corn must also be planted, or sown, in a rectangular block. This is because the plants carry both male and female flowers. The males are right at the top of the plant and the females, which are lower down, are recognized by the long silky hairs that hang from an oval, pointed, green sheath. If sweet corn is planted in a single row the very light pollen from the male flowers is blown away from the female flowers and there is a failure of cross-pollination. By block-planting, some pollen from the males will find a receptive female near at hand, no matter from what direction the wind is blowing.

The cobs are ready for gathering when the silky hairs or 'tassels' turn colour to deep, dark brown. To further check for ripeness, peel back the sheath and press your thumb into one of the golden-yellow grains. If it oozes a milky liquid it is not quite ready, but if the extraction should have the consistency

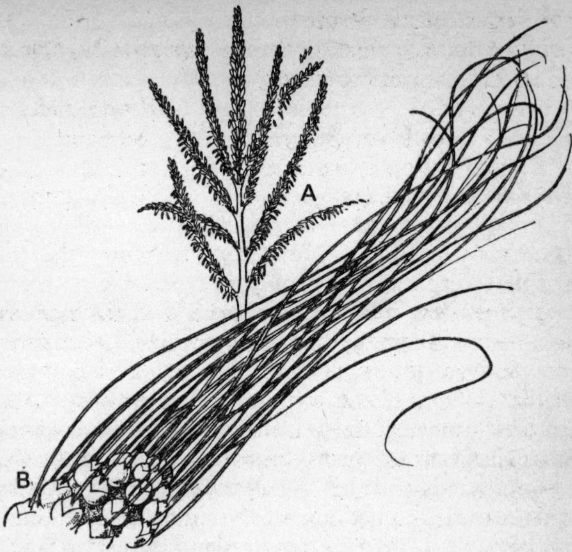

Sweetcorn showing male and female flowers:
A male flowers
B female flowers (the silks)

of clotted cream, cut the cob where it joins the stalk, boil, butter and enjoy it.

Good varieties: Aztec, Kelvedon Glory, North Star (all are F_1 hybrids)
Pests and/or diseases: frit fly
Blanching time: 4 to 8 minutes (depending on size)

Exhibition points: (cobs should be straight and fresh, with straight rows of undamaged grains)	Condition	5
	Form	3
	Setting of grain	4
	Uniformity	3
		15

Tomato

When it first arrived in Britain, around the beginning of the seventeenth century, the tomato was grown purely as a decorative plant. Now it has risen in popularity to become the most important greenhouse plant in cultivation. It is also being increasingly and successfully grown outdoors in the open ground and in a variety of containers. When it is well treated and generously fed, one tomato plant will yield up to 9 kg (20 lb) of delicious fruit.

Growing tomatoes outdoors

It used to be thought that only specially bred varieties would grow and crop outdoors. Nowadays, we know that many varieties that were once grown only in greenhouses also do well in the open garden. The main problem with outdoor-grown tomatoes it to get them to ripen in our uncertain climate. After growing many varieties in many different ways and places, I believe that the best results are obtained by growing them in a container positioned at the foot of a south-facing wall or fence. In such a situation the plants enjoy a fair amount of shelter from strong winds and they get all the available sunshine. In addition the wall, or fence, absorbs warmth during the day and retains a part of it to keep the tomato plants cosy at night. I have also tried various types of containers, and, without doubt, growing bags give the best and surest results. I find it is an advantage to grow the dwarf, bush varieties outdoors as they need less staking and I get more ripe tomatoes than I do from the taller-growing kinds.

My growing plan roughly follows these lines. I sow seeds of two bush tomatoes, such as The Amateur, Sigmabush or Pixie, in a heated propagator, temperature 18°C (65°F), in late March. The seeds are sown two to a 7-cm (3-in.) pot and if both germinate the weaker seedling is removed. I do not pot-on but feed with Phostrogen solution after the four-leaf stage. The growing bags are put in position in late April and are covered with Stewart cloches which, happily, are a perfect fit. Two to three weeks later, when the compost in the bags has warmed under the cloches, the tomatoes are planted, three to the large-size bag. The cloches are immediately replaced, together with end-pieces, and stay in place until the plants are touching the tops in June. During this period they are watered when necessary, but no feed is given until the first truss shows several open flowers.

Care and commonsense are needed when watering plants in growing bags. As there are no drainage holes overwatering is a distinct possibility, especially when the plants are small and are losing little water by transpiration. Bush tomatoes are prolific growers and, unless they are checked, they grow more branches than they can usefully manage. I have found that if I restrict the plants to three main branches and stop all subsequent laterals after that, on both main stem and laterals, I get bigger, better, earlier and riper tomatoes. Therefore, once the main branches have been established, all secondary laterals arising from the union of stem and branch are pinched out between finger and thumb. The bushy plants reach an eventual height of about 45 cm (18 in.) and they need a short 60 cm (2 ft) stake to each branch, otherwise the weight of the laden trusses may cause the branches to snap at their bases. When the second truss is beginning to show sizeable fruit, I step up the liquid feeding from once weekly to once every five days, to meet the plants' increasing demand for nutrients.

Using this growing system, about two-thirds of the fruits ripen by the end of the season. The green tomatoes remaining on the bushes are either picked to make a very tasty chutney, or they are put away in drawers to ripen in their own time.

Tomatoes can also be grown outdoors in the soil. It should be rich in fertilizers, especially in well-rotted manure, or compost, dug in early in the year. Never, ever, use fresh, uncomposted manure for tomatoes, they dislike it intensely. Some tall tomato varieties also do well outdoors. They are treated in the same way as those grown in greenhouses, except that they are not normally allowed to carry more than four or five trusses of fruits.

Greenhouse tomatoes

There is a very wide choice of greenhouse tomato varieties and in general the F_1 hybrids give the best crops. The varieties I have listed are those that I and a few colleagues have grown and deemed to be the best for cropping and for flavour. In the greenhouse there are three main growing methods – in beds, in bottomless rings and in growing bags.

The bed system

The bed system was once the only method used for growing greenhouse tomatoes. The plants were planted in beds 60 cm (2 ft) apart in fertile soil and later fed with liquid fertilizer drawn off from bags of manure steeped in water. The system gave good results for about three years, then the quality of growth and of fruiting potential deteriorated rapidly, and sometimes the plants wilted and died. When this happened the old gardeners pronounced the soil 'tomato-sick'. The sickness was due, usually, to either a build-up of soil toxicity, or to the increasing incidence of soil pests. It was, therefore, the custom to remove the soil in the bed to a depth of 45 to 60 cm (1½ to 2 ft), replacing it with fresh soil from the garden. Commercial growers surmounted the problem by steam-sterilizing their tomato beds annually, something the amateur could not do.

For those who still grow greenhouse tomatoes in beds, there are chemical soil sterilants now available. These are applied during the winter months, when the beds are empty, but in my experience the chemicals tend to taint the fruit and I prefer not to use them. As I had also grown weary of the laborious task of changing the soil every three years, I quickly changed to the 'ring culture' method of cultivation when it appeared.

The ring culture system

In its simplest terms, the ring culture system involves growing tomatoes, either in a no-soil medium that is sterile, or in one that can be easily renewed annually.

The sterile medium system entails digging out and removing the existing soil in the bed, to a depth of 30 cm (12 in.) The resulting trench is then lined with polythene sheeting along the bottom and up the sides. This is done to isolate the sub-soil and any pests it may harbour from the growing medium. On to the polythene base is put a 15-cm (6-in.) layer of coarse gravel or weathered clinker and the remaining space is filled with a fairly fine, '5 mm down' grit or gravel. The term '5 mm down' means that no particle is more than 5 mm (¼ in.) in diameter.

Ring culture of tomatoes; the top ring stands on peat, the lower two on gravel.

The bed is now ready for the bottomless rings. These are 20 cm (9 in.) diameter, pliable rings, without bottoms, that last for one year only. The rings are spaced out, 60 cm (2 ft) apart, on the gravel bed and filled to within 2 cm (1 in.) of their rims with John Innes No. 3 potting compost. The filling is done a week or two before planting, to warm the compost to greenhouse temperature. The tomato plants are then planted firmly, one to a pot and watered well in. This is the one and only time that water is poured into the ring. From now onwards the gravel, commonly referred to as the 'aggregate', is kept thoroughly wet and the plant roots soon find their way down into it. For the duration of their existence the tomatoes derive their water supply from the aggregate.

Canes, or taut twine, suspended from cross-wires are put in position to support the growing plants. When the flowers on the first truss set and small tomatoes are seen forming, regular feeding begins. For feeding use a specific tomato fertilizer with a high potash content and apply the solution into the ring itself. The tomato plant now has two root systems each with a task to perform. In the aggregate the roots absorb water, whilst the roots in the ring are concerned only with feeding. At first, feed once a week, but once the plants are past the three-truss stage, step up the feeding to once every three or four days.

The bigger the plant and the more trusses it has to carry, the more food it needs to sustain it. Remove all side shoots from the leaf axils with a sharp knife and pick the ripe tomatoes regularly to encourage continuous fruiting. At the end of the season, remove the plants to the compost heap, throw the spent John Innes compost on the garden and soak the aggregate with Jeyes' Fluid to kill off lurking pests.

The renewable growing medium is a modified version of the sterile medium system (*see* illustration on p. 135). The only difference is that a shallow 15 cm (6 in.) deep trench is excavated, lined with polythene and filled with peat. Bottomless rings are filled with peat-based compost and spaced out 60 cm (2 ft) apart on the bed of peat. Watering, feeding and growing techniques are the same as for the sterile medium system. At the end of the season the plants are discarded and the peat and compost can be used in the garden as fertilizers.

Seed sowing dates for tomatoes intended for greenhouse cultivation depend entirely on the level of heat provided. Tomato seeds need, ideally, 18°C (65°F) to germinate and a temperature of at least between 12°C to 15°C (55°F to 60°F) for growing on. If the temperatures fall below this level the plants take on a bluish look, a sure indication that they are experiencing a growth check. Plants checked in this way never fully recover and their crop potential is permanently impaired. So unless you can provide the heat necessary to maintain the critical temperatures in the early part of the year, wait until the end of March before sowing. Your crop will ripen later but you will, at least, be assured of a good return for money and effort.

The growing-bag system

Tomatoes in greenhouses are increasingly and very successfully being grown in growing-bags. Here again watering and feeding are controlled and the danger of soil pests is totally eliminated. After use the contents of the bags make a useful fertilizer for the garden. It is not uncommon for one growing bag containing three tomato plants to yield in the region of 27 kg (60 lb) of fruit in a season; a good yield by any standards.

Finally, the best tips I can give for growing tomatoes under glass are, keep the air moving and be careful with watering. Tomatoes must have a fresh, buoyant atmosphere, otherwise they are very susceptible to a number of fungus diseases. Whenever possible, water in the morning so that the plants have aerial humidity during the day and comparatively dry air at night. Watering late in the day results in heavy condensation inside the greenhouse, when outside temperatures drop. These are the very conditions that invite fungus attack. Shade the plants in high summer by painting the outside of the house with limewash, or 'greening liquid', or by fitting sun blinds. Above all water and feed the plants consistently and never let them meet dry root conditions.

Good varieties:

Outdoor:

(a) Bush varieties – Pixie, The Amateur, Sigmabush (an F_1 hybrid)

(b) Tall varieties – Gemini (an F_1 hybrid), Alicante, Moneymaker, Ailsa Craig

Greenhouse: Grenadier, Gemini, Eurocross A (all F_1 hybrids), Alicante, Ailsa Craig, Golden Sunrise

Pests and/or diseases: aphids, blight, blossom-end rot, grey mould, root rot

Exhibition points:	Condition	6
(fruits should be firm, round,	Colour	4
well-coloured, but not over-ripe,	Size	4
with calyces (sepals) attached)	Form	4
		18

Turnip (brassica group)

Turnips are closely allied to swedes and appreciate similar cultivation. Seeds are sown, in succession, from March to April for summer roots and again in July and early August to provide roots for winter storage and use. Sow in drills set 20 cm (9 in.) apart and thin the seedlings to 15 to 20 cm (6 to 9 in.) apart. For summer use, lift the turnips when they are at their best, which is when they are about the size of a billiard ball. For winter use, lift the roots in October before frost can damage them and store them in sand or peat.

Good varieties: Golden Ball, Red Top Milan, Snowball
Pests and/or diseases: *see under* Swede (p. 129)
Blanching time: 2 to 3 minutes (diced)

Exhibition points:	Condition	6
(roots should be unmarked, of	Size and	
medium size, solid and shapely	solidity	5
with small tap-roots)	Uniformity	4
		15

HERBS

There is no doubt that people who make good use of herbs in their cooking, lead healthier, happier lives than those who don't. Modern medicinal drugs are often indispensable for effecting cures when diseases have already struck, but a diet of fresh vegetables, supported by herbs, is the best preventive.

Indeed, many herbs possess powerful curative properties as well. I believe I owe my life to herbs. In my early youth it was discovered that I was afflicted with the first symptoms of the then dreaded T.B. I was whisked off to visit a veteran herbalist, who diagnosed the problem just by peering at me through an impressive pair of horn-rimmed spectacles. Following his diagnosis he scuttled from the room to return, some minutes later, bearing a large brown paper parcel that turned out to contain a mysterious mixture of herb leaves and seeds. My mother was instructed to make a 'tea' from the daunting concoction and to feed it to me daily until the bag was empty.

For many weeks I suffered a nightly dose of liquid 'compost' and I can still taste the vile and shuddering flavour. Eventually, and not a moment too soon for my liking, the paper-bag was empty and my lungs were once more in perfect working order. Senna pods also figured largely in my young life. Every Friday night I was submitted to a revolting cupful of senna tea to purify my alimentary canal. This it did with regular efficiency. It may be said that I suffered unwillingly in the cause of good health. I attribute my subsequent well-being to my early involvement with herbal remedies and to their continued use in our everyday diet in the home.

In the garden I grow a variety of herbs that my wife uses constantly in the kitchen. The herb bed measures a mere 1.8 × 1.2 metres (6 × 4 ft), yet it is big enough to house all the herbs we need, because a little goes a long way. A few leaves are enough to impart a delicate flavour to a variety of dishes. One rosemary bush, one sage and two or three clumps of thyme, for instance, will provide enough all-the-year-round snippets for the average family.

Nearly all herbs may be grown easily from seeds, providing they are sown according to whether they are hardy or half-hardy, annual or perennial. If they are hardy they may be sown direct into the herb bed and later thinned to the appropriate distances apart. Half-hardy herbs are sown in a propagator or greenhouse and planted out, when the risk of frost is over. Annual herbs have a life span of one year only and therefore have to be renewed annually from seed. Perennial herbs, if they are hardy, will last for several years, especially when they are being constantly pruned for kitchen use. However, if you find that a particular clump of herbs is showing signs of decline, it is time to replace it with new stock that can be readily raised from seeds or cuttings. In fact, many herbs, such as sage and marjoram, seed themselves freely. Allow them to flower and form seed, then look under the clumps where you will usually find seedlings that may be lifted and transplanted to new ground.

People without gardens need not be deprived of the incomparable flavour of fresh herbs. Many of the low-growing kinds may be grown in pots, window-boxes (either indoors or out) and all do well in growing bags on patios and like places. In very small gardens, where a separate herb bed may be difficult to site, many herbs may be planted to augment the decorative display. For instance, borage has pretty blue flowers that attract the bees and butterflies from miles around, and the lilac-blue flowers of chives make a perfect edging for a small herbaceous border.

I must make special mention of two invaluable herbs – mint and garlic. There are several varieties of mint, and having tried most of them the best-flavoured, without doubt, is *Mentha rotundifolia*, the apple mint. It has large, roundish and slightly hairy leaves and imparts a subtle mint and apple flavour. Like all mints it is invasive. Planted in a bed or border its roots spread far and wide and the original plants rapidly become a nuisance, have to be lifted and their intrusion curtailed. The best plan is to plant mint in a large pot, or an old, leaky bucket, where its rampant growth can be kept in check.

I single out garlic for special mention for two reasons. Firstly, it is grown from 'bulbs' rather than from seeds and secondly it has tremendous dietary importance. The garlic bulb that you buy is a composite structure, made up of several bulblets or cloves, the whole being covered in a white, parchment-like skin. To plant, separate the cloves and plant them individually, 5 cm (2 in.) deep and 20 cm (9 in.) apart. When the tall stem and leaves have withered and died, lift the new 'bulbs' wth a fork and dry and store them in the same way as onions. The role of garlic in the kitchen is twofold. Used moderately it imparts a superb and subtle flavour to curries, pickles, meat and many other dishes. Unfortunately, the aroma of garlic hangs on the breath for a long time after it is eaten, to the dismay of friends and associates who dislike its pungent flavour. However, its after-effects can be countered by chewing a few sprigs of parsley immediately after a garlic-spiced meal. Garlic is also one of the best, natural blood purifiers in the world and was even used during the 1914–18 war as a dressing on wounds to prevent gangrene.

TABLE OF USEFUL HERBS

Name	Type	Height	Average number of plants required	Principal uses	Notes
Angelica	Biennial	1.5m (5ft)	2-3	Stems are used for candying and in tarts and jams. Dried leaves are used in pot-pourri.	Sow outdoors in May to obtain plants for use in the following year.
Balm	Perennial	60cm (2ft)	1-2	Imparts a lemon flavour to iced drinks and cooked dishes.	Leaves are dark green and smell of lemon when crushed.
Basil (sweet)	Half-hardy annual	30cm (1ft)	2-3	A good flavouring for egg, meat, fish and especially tomato dishes.	Sow in warmth in March or outdoors in mid-May.
Borage	Hardy annual	60cm (2ft)	2-3	Leaves have a cool, cucumber flavour in salads, wine cups and are very good with cooked cabbage.	Sow outdoors in April and May. Blue flowers attract bees.
Coriander	Hardy annual	90cm (3ft)	3-6	Seeds are used to flavour curries, pickles, lamb, pork, sauces and stuffings and in apple pie.	A lovely feathery plant. Sow outdoors in April and May.
Chives	Perennial	30-45cm (1-1½ft)	Short unthinned rows	Mild onion flavour. Very good chopped into salads and in sandwich fillings and sauces.	May be grown as an edging to beds and borders. Flower heads are lilac-blue.

Dill	Hardy annual	90cm (3ft)	Grow a row to suit your needs	Leaves for flavouring fish, vegetables and for pickling cucumbers. Seeds for flavouring soups, fish, lamb, stews, cooked cabbage and vegetable salads.	Sow in succession from April to the end of June.
Fennel(sweet)	Perennial	2m (7ft)	1-2	Used in salads, as a flavouring for fish sauces, and in gripe water and for treating sore eyes.	Fine, feathery leaves that have a pleasant smell of aniseed.
Hyssop	Perennial	60cm (2ft)	1	Imparts a bitter, minty flavour and is used sparingly in salads and with meat, soups and stews. It improves the taste of honey.	Has attractive blue flowers. A good plant for the herbaceous border.
Lovage	Perennial	1.2m (4ft)	1-2	Leaves have a taste like celery. Used in soups, stews, casseroles and salads.	Tall plants needing a lot of room and a deep, fertile soil. Sow in May.
Marjoram	Perennial	60cm (2ft)	2-3	A herb for meat dishes, with a spicy flavour. Especially good for flavouring sausages.	Sow seeds in March-April or take cuttings in early summer.
Mint	Perennial	60-120cm (2-4ft)	Clump	For flavouring mutton and lamb, iced drinks, liqueurs and mint tea.	Grow mint in an old bucket or large pot to prevent it spreading. Apple mint is a particularly good variety.

Name	Type	Height	Average number of plants required	Principal uses	Notes
Rosemary	Perennial	1.2m (4ft)	1-2	Imparts a fine flavour to all kinds of dishes, very good with lamb. Also used in cider drinks and for making shortbread biscuits.	A very decorative, scented shrub with pale, lavender-blue flowers. An asset in the shrub border.
Sage	Perennial	60-90cm (2-3ft)	1-2	Used in stuffings, soups and stews.	Rather loose growth that needs regular cutting to keep the plants bushy.
Tarragon	Perennial	60-90cm (2-3ft)	1-2	Bitter-sweet flavour, ideal for sauces, stuffings and for shell-fish, especially lobster. Also makes tarragon vinegar.	Use sparingly, as a little goes a long way.
Thyme	Perennial	15cm (6in)	2-3	Excellent for stuffings and for cooking fatty meats such as pork.	Plants need replacing every three years or so. Makes a good edging plant.
Savory (summer)	Hardy annual	30cm (1ft)	1-2	Aids the digestion. Used for flavouring french and runner beans and salads.	There is also a winter savory that is perennial and has a stronger flavour.

7

PUTTING YOUR TROUBLES BEHIND YOU

No matter how careful we are or how well we grow our vegetables, pests are always with us. Weeds will inevitably appear; indeed I would be worried if they didn't, as I would suspect the fertility of my soil. A variety of insects enjoy our vegetables just as much as we do and there are fungus spores in the air to descend on our crops. But, take heart, they do not all attack and decimate together and there are ways and means of dealing with those that do.

Before dealing in detail with the pests that we are likely to meet, let me emphasize a few basic, indisputable truths. The stronger we grow our vegetables, the better able they are to withstand and combat the enemy, which brings us back to the vital importance of high soil fertility. Also the vigour inherent in F_1 hybrids renders them less susceptible to pests than ordinary varieties. Therefore, wherever possible, buy and sow F_1 hybrids, even though their seeds cost a few pence more. Finally, a word of warning. There are organic and inorganic chemicals on the market that prevent and destroy most of the pests that beset us. Of the two I prefer to use the organic controls, because they are derived from plants and are unlikely to harm either wild life, pets, or humans. The two organic insecticides in common use are derris and pyrethrum. Unfortunately, these alone are not the panacea for all our ills and from time to time we have to resort to inorganic chemical pesticides. Those available have been thoroughly tested for their efficiency and safety by the manufacturers and, as far as it is possible to ascertain, there is no risk involved in their use, with one proviso: the manufacturer's instructions on the pack *must* be followed to the letter. Always stick to the recommended solution strength otherwise you may damage your plants, or you may render the treatment totally ineffectual. Always wash your hands and face when you have finished and also thoroughly wash the spraying or watering equipment. If you have used a watering-can rinse it at least four times and do the same with the sprayer. In fact, I think it worth investing in a second watering-can that is kept purely for weedkillers and pesticides; it avoids the risk of killing cultivated plants by any residual chemicals left in the can normally used for watering. Also check the instructions to see whether the pesticide is safe to use on all plants. There are some pesticides, for instance, that are lethal to all members of the cucumber family. Finally and most importantly, never put any pesticide solution in any container that does not clearly identify the contents and keep everything well out of the reach of children. Remember that chemical pesticides are lethal to insects, fungus diseases and to humans, so handle them properly and with respect.

Weedkillers

The hoe is still the best and safest weedkiller. Used regularly, once a week, during the growing season it kills weed seedlings before they get big enough to choke crops and before they can deprive the soil of valuable expensive nutrients.

In the vegetable garden weedkillers may be grouped into those that are (a) root absorbed, (b) leaf absorbed, (c) persistent and (d) non-persistent.

Sodium chlorate

Sodium chlorate is old-fashioned having been largely superseded by improved weedkillers. It is absorbed through the roots and kills the entire plant. It has two big disadvantages. It is persistent and can remain active in the soil for several months. Therefore ground cleared of weed growth with sodium chlorate is useless for vegetable growing for up to 12 months; the heavier the soil, the longer the toxicity period. It is also invasive by virtue of its high solubility. In other words, if a solution of sodium chlorate is applied to a particular area of ground, it will spread laterally for some distance, possibly killing cherished plants in its path.

Simazine-based weedkillers

These weedkillers are comparable in all respects to sodium chlorate with one important difference. In water they become suspensions rather than solutions and are, therefore, not invasive; they do not spread laterally, but they are persistent. They are ideal for keeping garden paths free of weeds for a whole season, from one application in early spring.

Paraquat-based weedkillers

These weedkillers are non-persistent and kill plants by absorption through the leaves. They are, therefore, only effective when weeds are in leaf. They dispose of annual and shallow-rooted perennial weeds very quickly and totally. Deep-rooted perennial weeds need more than one treatment before the kill is complete. The first application will destroy the top growth, but secondary growth will shortly appear. This should be given a further application, while the leaves are young and soft. Applications of paraquat are most effective applied early in the day in dry weather. It should be remembered that paraquat is not selective, it kills all green plants it touches but it is non-persistent in the soil. Therefore use it with care and preferably with a dribble-bar attached to the can nozzle. A dribble-bar gives greater control and a more economical distribution of the weedkiller solution. Note also that it is highly poisonous to humans.

Glyphosate-based weedkillers

Glyphosate works in exactly the same way as paraquat and appears to be more effective in controlling deep-rooted weeds, such as docks and dandelions. It penetrates the plant from leaf to root tip and therefore second applications are seldom necessary. It is slow-acting and may take three weeks, or longer, to despatch strong, established weeds. Like paraquat, it is non-persistent and treated ground may safely be planted about three weeks after treatment.

Pesticides

Insect pests fall broadly into two categories – the suckers and the chewers. The sucking insects, such as greenfly, weaken plants by extracting sap from their leaves and stems, whereas the chewers, such as caterpillars, eat large areas of the leaves and thus deprive plants of vital parts of their food-manufacturing surfaces.

Insecticides

These may also be split into two categories – the contact killers and the systemic killers. A contact insecticide kills when it touches the pest and it does not discriminate between friend and enemy. If an amiable bee or ladybird passes by when you are spraying the greenfly on your roses, they, too, will meet their deaths. As its name implies, a systemic insecticide is absorbed through the leaves into the plant's circulatory system. When the insect sucks the sap it also imbibes a dose of lethal insecticide. A systemic insecticide is, therefore, specific and only kills the insect pests attacking treated plants. As with all garden chemicals a number of precautions are necessary when you are spraying with insecticides:

(a) Spray on still, windless days, so that the atomized mist does not drift into neighbouring gardens and on to other crops.
(b) Spray with, rather than against, the moving air. In other words, avoid the spray drifting back on to your face and into your lungs.
(c) Spray on dull, cloudy days to avoid the risk of scorching the leaves.
(d) Hold the sprayer, or aerosol, about 60 cm (2 ft) away from the leaves and spray in short bursts. It is not necessary to soak the leaves to kill the insects, a few drops will do the trick.
(e) Wash all exposed skin immediately spraying is finished and rinse the equipment several times to remove all chemical traces.
(f) Make sure you spray at the right time as advised by the manufacturer. For example it is inadvisable to spray fruit trees when the flowers are fully open and pollination is taking place.
(g) Do not eat vegetables that have been sprayed, or dusted, until it is safe to do so. Where applicable, the manu-

facturer's on-pack instructions will advise on how many days should elapse between treatment and consumption.

Fungicides
Most vegetables are host to some fungus disease or other. The fungus seeds, or spores, are airborne. They descend on the leaves of the host plant and literally root into the leaf tissue, eventually causing total destruction. In general, fungus growth flourishes in warm, humid, still-air conditions, so try to grow your plants in a fresh, buoyant atmosphere. When you spot trouble, remove and burn affected plants and start treatment immediately to prevent the disease spreading.

As with insecticides, fungicides are also either contact or systemic killers and all the advice and precautions previously mentioned apply.

Pests and diseases often encountered
Now for a short resume of the pests and diseases most commonly encountered in the vegetable plot, together with advice on appropriate chemical treatments. In most cases the chemical in question will be sold under a manufacturer's trade name, but if you read the information given on the packs you will find the constituent chemicals listed.

Troubles, hosts and treatments

Aphids: lettuce, tomatoes, broad and runner beans and other crops.

Aphids include greenfly, blackfly and mealy aphid. Blackfly on broad beans may be controlled by pinching out the growing tips of the plants when they are in flower. Otherwise spray with formothion, malathion or pirimicarb.

Asparagus beetle: asparagus.

The leaves and stems are eaten. Spray with derris or malathion.

Blight: potatoes, tomatoes.

Yellowish-brown patches appear on the leaves and they

eventually rot. Spray with Bordeaux mixture, maneb or zineb. In areas where blight is troublesome, it is a wise precaution to spray maincrop potatoes in early July.

Blossom end rot: tomatoes.

Container-grown tomatoes are the most susceptible. Brownish-black circular patches appear on the bottom of the fruits. Blossom end rot is not a disease, but a condition brought about by insufficient water at the roots, i.e. allowing the compost to dry out from time to time.

Botrytis (*see* Grey mould).

Cabbage root fly: all brassica crops (including swedes and turnips).

Eggs are laid around the stem at soil level. The maggots that hatch out eat their way down the stem. First signs of trouble are wilting and the leaves assume a bluish look. Dust the planting holes and soil surface with bromophos at planting time. Established plants suffering attack may be watered with diazinon or trichlorphon solutions.

Canker: parsnips.

The roots show a reddish-brown rot around the shoulders, which may eventually cause the entire root to rot. There is no known, effective treatment at present, but the condition is less likely to occur where crop rotation is practised, by sowing very early or very late and by growing resistant varieties.

Carrot root fly: carrots, parsnips, parsley.

The carrot fly attacks carrots in the same way as the cabbage fly attacks brassicas. The leaves appear a reddish-yellow green and may wilt. Treat with bromophos or diazonin, by dusting into the drills after sowing. Late May and early June sowings will usually escape attack as the fly lays its eggs in early May and again in late August.

Caterpillars: all brassica crops, sweet peppers.

The leaves are eaten and in severe attacks may be reduced to a mere latticework of veins. Spray or dust with derris or trichlorphon.

Club root: all brassica crops (including swedes and turnips).

Club root is a severe and persistent fungus disease. Once it gets a hold it is transmitted in the soil from one year to the next. The disease is not seed-borne, so the best course is to grow your own plants from seed and never buy or accept plants that may have infected soil around their roots. If you already have club root in your garden I suggest the following treatment.

1. Apply ground chalk, or limestone to the brassica bed, at between 340 to 450 grams (12 to 16 oz) to the square metre, if your soil is acid.

Dipping brassica roots in 4% calomel paste before planting

2. When planting dip the roots in a thick paste of 4 per cent calomel dust mixed with water.
3. I have evidence that a moth-ball put into each planting hole is an effective remedy; at least twenty 'ancients' have told me it works.

Damping-off: all seedlings.

The fungus disease damping-off affects seedlings that are overcrowded, are in an over-wet soil, or are growing in a very humid atmosphere. The stems are attacked at soil level and the seedlings topple over and die. The best prevention is to sow thinly, to thin early, to give just enough water, and, in the greenhouse, to provide good ventilation. Treat affected seedlings with Cheshunt Compound or zineb.

Downy mildew: lettuce, onion, spinach.

On lettuce and spinach the fungus causes yellow blotches on the upper surfaces of the leaves. On onions, the leaves turn a greyish colour, then wither and die. Spray with zineb or dust with Bordeaux powder.

Eelworm: potato, onion, peas and beans, tomatoes, leek.

There are several species of eelworm that attack the roots of their own particular host plant. A regular crop rotation system reduces the risk of infection, but there is no chemical deterrent readily available to the amateur. Commercially, a soil-sterilant called dazomet achieves a good degree of control.

Flea beetle: all brassicas.

All brassicas are affected although the insect is usually more active on swedes and turnips. Seedling leaves are pitted with pin-prick holes and their growth seriously retarded. Treat with derris.

Foot and root rots: peas and beans, celery, tomatoes.

Foot and root rots are caused by a variety of soil pests that flourish in poor soil conditions. Avoid by re-siting the crops every year and treat with Cheshunt Compound or zineb, at the first sign of rotting at the base of the stems.

Grey mould (botrytis): cucumber, tomato, marrow, pumpkin, lettuce.

A greyish-brown fungal growth appears on the leaves and on the stems, and fruits, in the case of fruiting plants. Good hygiene is the best preventive. Remove and burn all affected leaves and spray with thiram.

Leaf miner: celery, celeriac.

The larvae of the celery fly live within the leaf tissue causing them to turn yellow, shrivel and die. Spray with trichlorphon or dimethoate.

Leaf spot: celery, brassica crops, spinach, peas and beans, beetroot.

This fungus disease is a symptom of soft growth often due to applying too much nitrogenous fertilizer, especially in a wet season. Practise crop rotation and apply sulphate of potash next time round.

Mealy aphid: brassica crops.

Mealy aphid is easily recognized by the revolting grey deposit on the underside of brassica leaves and on the edible parts of Brussels sprouts, cauliflower and broccoli. Spray under the leaves with dimethoate or formothion.

Mildew (*see* Downy mildew and Powdery mildew).

Neck rot: onion.

This disease is not evident until the onions have been lifted and stored, so inspect the bulbs regularly and remove and burn any showing a grey mould on or near the neck. To prevent attack harvest and dry the bulbs well and store them in a cool, dry and airy place.

Onion fly: onion, garlic, shallot, chives, leek.

The maggots of the onion fly enter the bulbs causing the leaves to turn yellow and fall over. Onions grown from sets are less liable to attack than those grown from seeds. Treat the soil with a pesticide such as diazinon or bromophos at planting or sowing time.

Pea moth: pea.

The moth lays its eggs when the peas are in flower. When the eggs hatch the caterpillars tunnel into the pods and feed on the developing peas inside. Spray with fenitrothion a week after the plants start flowering, between June and mid-August. Early varieties, in flower before June, escape attack.

Pea and bean weevil: peas and broad beans.

A common insect pest that eats U-shaped holes in the margins of the leaves. Damage is most serious and severe when young seedlings are attacked and their growth checked. Dust with H.C.H. (formerly known as B.H.C.) at the first signs of damage.

Powdery mildew: cucumber, marrow, pumpkin.

The leaves appear covered with a white floury dust. It is usually associated with dryness at the roots. Spray with benomyl or dinocap.

Red spider: French and runner beans.

The red spider spends its life on the undersides of the leaves and is only just visible to the perceptive, naked eye. Affected leaves are discoloured and in severe attacks the plants die. Spray with malathion or formothion at seven-day intervals.

Rust: leek, mint.

Leaves show bright orange marks. There are no chemical deterrents, so destroy affected plants and change the leek plot around every year.

Scab: potato, beetroot, radish.

The skins of the roots or tubers are 'scabby' and unsightly. The condition, however, is only skin deep and the crops remain perfectly edible. Scab is more likely to occur in stony or gravelly ground, or where the soil has been recently limed. Prevent attack by digging in plenty of 'organics', and, in the case of potatoes, plant the tubers on a layer of manure or compost and put a second layer over them. There is no other treatment.

Slugs: practically all plants.

Some slugs eat leaves, others will devour root crops such as potatoes. To dispel surface slugs put down slug pellets as bait and renew it from time to time. Subterranean slugs are more difficult to deal with. There are small 'grains' available that may be scattered in the drills at planting time and a dose of Jeyes Fluid at horticultural strength is also a deterrent. A very light dusting of copper sulphate in the drills when planting will prevent the small keel slugs from causing damage to potatoes.

White fly: brassicas and greenhouse crops.

The white fly is a tough and persistent insect. Its larvae live under the leaves and suck the sap thus causing a severe growth check. It is active all the year round and will survive the hardest winter. Spray every five to seven days with resmethrin, bioresmethrin or dimethoate.

Pressure-spraying cabbages

White rot: onion family.

White rot starts at the base of the bulbs while they are in the ground. The leaves turn yellow and die. Examine the onion bed regularly from early July onwards and remove and burn any plants that are infected. Prevent attack by practising crop rotation and dust the drills with 4 per cent calomel dust when sowing or planting.

Wireworm: potatoes, carrots.

Wireworms are usually only really troublesome in ground that was until recently pastureland. Regular cultivation steadily reduces their numbers; also treat the soil with bromophos or diazinon at planting time.

Tomato virus.

The tomato is prone to attack by a number of viruses that cause discoloration and mottling of the leaves, stems and fruit. The growth of the plants is also severely stunted. There is no effective treatment except to destroy all affected plants and to practise a high standard of cleanliness in the greenhouse.

AFTERWORD

I have grown vegetables all my life. After nearly 40 years of relaxed tilling and toiling I still find few satisfactions to compare with the thrill of seeing empty ground become studded with lines of young vegetable seedlings in spring. The excitement continues and grows as the vegetables approach maturity – lettuces and cabbages heart up, onions begin to swell, peas and beans flower and pod, and runner beans scamper up their canes. The time comes when I harvest the fruits of my labours – an abundance of fresh, tasty and untainted vegetables, produced at low cost and with great pleasure.

INDEX

Page numbers in italics indicate illustrations

Prices and postage and packing rates shown below were correct at the time of going to press.

FICTION

All prices shown are exclusive of postage and packing.

GENERAL FICTION

☐ THE AFFAIR OF NINA B.	Simmel	£1.20
☐ H.M.S. BOUNTY	John Maxwell	£1.00
☐ TY-SHAN BAY	R. T. Aundrews	95p
☐ A SEA CHANGE	Lois Gould	80p
☐ THE PLAYERS	Gary Brandner	95p
☐ MR. FITTON'S COMMISSION	Showell Styles	85p
☐ CRASH LANDING	Mark Regan	95p
☐ SUMMER LIGHTNING	Judith Richards	£1.00
☐ THE HALO JUMP	Alistair Hamilton	£1.00
☐ SUMMERBLOOD	Anne Rudeen	£1.25
☐ PLACE OF THE DAWN	Gordon Taylor	90p
☐ EARTHLY POSSESSIONS	Anne Tyler	95p
☐ THE MASTER MECHANIC	I. G. Broat	£1.50
☐ THE MEXICAN PROPOSITION (Western)	Matt Chisholm	75p

CRIME/THRILLER

☐ THE TREMOR OF FORGERY	Patricia Highsmith	80p
☐ STRAIGHT	Steve Knickmeyer	80p
☐ THE COOL COTTONTAIL	John Ball	80p
☐ JOHNNY GET YOUR GUN	John Ball	85p
☐ CONFESS, FLETCH	Gregory Mcdonald	90p
☐ THE TRIPOLI DOCUMENTS	Henry Kane	95p
☐ THE EXECUTION	Oliver Crawford	90p
☐ TIME BOMB	James D. Atwater	90p
☐ THE SPECIALIST	Jasper Smith	85p
☐ KILLFACTOR FIVE	Peter Maxwell	85p
☐ ROUGH DEAL	Walter Winward	85p
☐ THE SONORA MUTATION	Albert J. Elias	85p
☐ THE RANSOM COMMANDO	James Grant	95p
☐ THE DESPERATE HOURS	Joseph Hayes	90p
☐ THE MOLE	Dan Sherman	95p

ROMANCE

☐ THE PROUD SERVANT	Margaret Irwin	£1.25
☐ THE GAY GALLIARD	Margaret Irwin	£1.25
☐ THE STRANGER PRINCE	Margaret Irwin	£1.25
☐ SO WICKED MY DESIRE	Stephanie Blake	£1.50
☐ MYSTIC ROSE	Patricia Gallagher	£1.20
☐ CAPTIVE BRIDE	Johanna Lindsey	£1.00
☐ A PIRATE'S LOVE	Johanna Lindsey	£1.20
☐ GILLIANE	Roberta Gellis	£1.50
☐ GREEN GIRL	Sandra Heath	80p
☐ THE TALL ONE	Barbara Jefferis	£1.00
☐ ROYAL MISTRESS	Patricia Campbell Horton	£1.50

SCIENCE FICTION

☐ THE OTHER LOG OF PHILEAS FOGG	Philip José Farmer	80p
☐ GRIMM'S WORLD	Vernor Vinge	75p
☐ A TOUCH OF STRANGE	Theodore Sturgeon	85p
☐ THE SILENT INVADERS	Robert Silverberg	80p
☐ THE SEED OF EARTH	Robert Silverberg	80p
☐ CRITICAL THRESHOLD	Brian M. Stableford	75p
☐ THE FLORIANS	Brian M. Stableford	80p
☐ FURY	Henry Kuttner	80p
☐ MUTANT	Henry Kuttner	90p
☐ HEALER	F. Paul Wilson	80p
☐ JOURNEY	Marta Randall	£1.00
☐ THE GAMEPLAYERS OF ZAN	M. A. Foster	£1.25
☐ PROJECT BARRIER	Daniel F. Galouye	80p
☐ THE MIND THING	Fredric Brown	90p
☐ THE PROUD ENEMY	F. M. Busby	90p

HORROR/OCCULT

☐ TRANCE	Joy Fielding	90p
☐ DEVIL'S COACH-HORSE	Richard Lewis	85p
☐ ISOBEL	Jane Parkhurst	£1.00
☐ RETURN OF THE HOWLING	Gary Brandner	85p
☐ RETURN OF THE LIVING DEAD	John Russo	80p
☐ DYING LIGHT	Evan Chandler	85p
☐ RATTLERS	Joseph L. Gilmore	85p
☐ LOCUSTS	Guy N. Smith	85p

FILM/TV TIE IN

☐ WUTHERING HEIGHTS	Emily Brontë	80p
☐ STAND ON IT	Stroker Ace	95p
☐ THE ROSE MEDALLION	James Grant	90p
☐ AMERICAN GIGOLO	Timothy Harris	90p